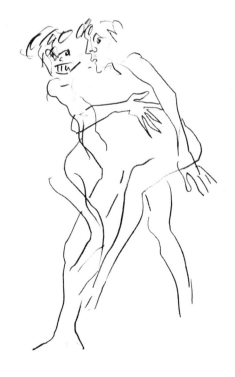

Karen Malpede # Three Works by

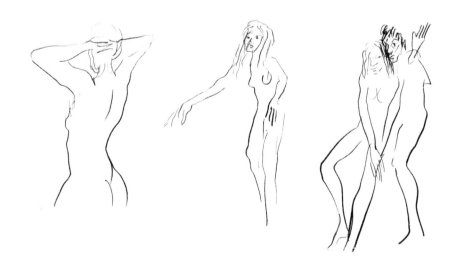

he Open Theater

The Company
Raymond Barry
Michael Bartuccio
Patricia Berman
Joseph Chaikin
Shami Chaikin
Gwen Fabricant
Ralph Lee
Tom Lillard
Ellen Maddow
Mira Rafalowicz
Stephen Rich
Jo Ann Schmidman
Sam Shepard
Tina Shepard
Roberta Sklar
John Stoltenberg
Megan Terry
Jean-Claude van Itallie
Susan Yankowitz
Paul Zimet

The Photographers
Mary Ellen Mark
Inge Morath
Max Waldman

Drawings by
Mary Frank

DRAMA BOOK SPECIALISTS/PUBLISHERS

Book design by Peretz Kaminsky

Library of Congress Cataloging in Publication Data

Open Theater
      Three works by the Open Theater.
      CONTENTS: Mutation show.—Nightwalk.—Terminal.
      1. American drama—20th century. I. Malpede,
Karen, ed. II. Chaikin, Joseph, 1935-   ed.
III. Title.
PS634.O65 1974   812'.5'408   74-13837
ISBN 0-910482-54-3

Printed in U.S.A. by
NOBLE OFFSET PRINTERS, INC.
New York, N.Y. 10003

Acknowledgments

John Stoltenberg and
Mira Rafalowicz helped
prepare the texts
for *The Mutation Show*
and *Nightwalk*.
Danny Kaiser edited
the introduction with
sympathy
and intelligence.

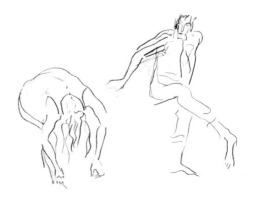

Contents

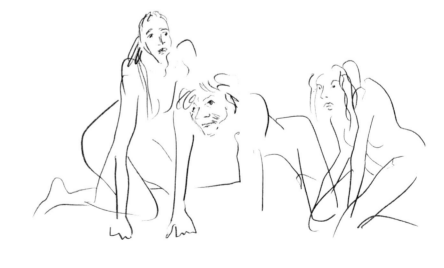

Introduction

It is manifest that behind the so-called
curtain, which is to hide the inner
world, there is nothing to be seen
unless we ourselves go behind there,
as much in order that we may thereby
see, as that there may be something
behind there which can be seen.

Hegel

The only counterforce [to fascism]
is the development of an effectively
organized radical Left, assuming the
vast task of *political education*, dis-
pelling the false and mutilated consciousness of the people so that they
themselves experience their condition
and its abolition, as vital need, and
apprehend the ways and means of
their liberation.

Marcuse

I want to talk about the Open Theater's work, not works, because I think they have made one of the great esthetic and ethical statements of our time. I think they not only looked harder and saw more, they found a way to transmit what they learned. I think they spoke for us.

Watching them perform was always personal and public. The two worlds met on their stage. The actors were messengers come into that space to report what is knowable about the unknown. It was as if they had slipped inside my head and lifted my imagination so that I might know it. Actually, they went into themselves, not me, and brought back a notion I could also grasp. Now there was a place in which we met the other in ourselves. This was the fact. It was also the intention. Joe Chaikin often said, "The actor is the audience in action."

The Open Theater did not disband because they could not do what they set out to do, but because what they set out to do is no longer enough. There is a greater vision at their end than was present at their beginning. Proof of the usefulness of art. Reason for our feeling blessed by it.

The attempt can no longer be simply to change the theater. The attempt must be to change life, and by changing the nature of life it is inevitable that the nature of the theater will change. Brecht wanted the theater to show that society could be altered. The Open Theater's esthetic is different. It is a witness to changed life, insofar as its makers have changed their lives and are able to present these changes to the audience. Brecht's idea that the theater can teach is not bypassed; it is lived out. But the experience is actual rather than theoretical. There is a difference between commenting on oppressive situations and turning the actor's body into a testimony to liberated ones — the difference between alienation and community. That's why the work the Open Theater helped start has only just begun.

What is the relationship of art to ideas? It's impossible to imagine the Open Theater existing without the writings of Herbert Marcuse, Simone Weil, or R. D. Laing. Yet it's equally impossible for me to imagine having come to such a real understanding of these intellectual statements without the presence of the Open Theater. A new esthetic

11

cannot exist without the ideas to challenge the logic of domination at every level. But ideas by themselves do not make a culture. One must know the situation emotionally and, perhaps primarily, physically. Unnecessary pain must be felt as unnecessary pain. Only at the moment when idea and experience correspond is it possible to change. To undo the tyranny of past and future one must first be present.

Conflict is called the essence of theater when theater pretends to be realistic. The conflict is between what the characters desire and what they are able to achieve once psychological and, occasionally, even economic limitations are considered. To act in this theater Stanislavsky developed a system of emotional recall which his followers then rigidified. The actor's energy is aroused by remembering past events from his or her life. Spontaneity is sacrificed to case history. The truthful response to every situation is supposed to have already been experienced. Plot pushed forward by reliance on the past becomes destiny. The actor, locked into his or her specific neuroses, is cut off from exploration and comes to stand for Alienated Man. The human condition is easily defined: people are naturally aggressive and want what they cannot have. The distance from this psychology to capitalism is not far. Capitalism separates the worker from the product of the work and externalizes the split between the wish and its fulfillment. Hope hovers around this world like a vulture, living off dying bodies and mutilated consciousness.

But another vision commands our attention more and more as it allows us to see some space around our lives. In the Open Theater's last three works the conflicts endemic to bourgeois theater have been replaced by contrasts. Conflict generates conflict, while contrast establishes the possibility of choice. Joe directs with a crucial question: "And now what's happening?" "And now what's happening?" He stops the actors at every moment a new choice is possible. And the Open Theater actors, led from the trap of causality, find other ways of being in this world. Extending the limits is always a matter of choice. Artistic creation is demystified if we keep this in mind. An artist is a person who has recognized each separate moment of choice. The truest discipline moves us in this direction. Community is the work of a group of people who become artists as they create the choices in their own lives. And we, with capitalism and no community, know the depth of our oppression by how difficult each choice has been: how hard it is to refuse to kill or to be killed, how difficult to control the quality of the air we breathe.

Out of the chaos of this existence the Open Theater arrived at a fragile freedom based on the proof that there are always two ways of being – the one we have been taught and the one we are learning. At any instant – but only with strict attention and highest energy – it is possible to move from one into the other.

This rite of passage becomes the obsession of our age because no other activity can go beyond simple recognition of economic oppression, psychological repression. Simultaneous exchange between the outer and the inner is the only posssible organizing myth, replacing history and the unconscious. For the Open Theater there was finally no other problem. In *Terminal, The Mutation Show* and *Nightwalk* they located the experiences most obscured by capitalist society and the realistic theater that represents it. Living/dying; transformation/socialization; waking/sleeping. Each term in each pair is at once the opposite of the other and a metaphoric comment on it. The pairs resonate off each other until we experience their meanings and arrive at a feeling of what a culture that nurtures the intellect and the imagination might be like. Joe would add that one duality most nearly describes the Open Theater's vision: presence/absence.

Yet the polarity is even more important than the meaning of the opposites. Each of The Open Theater's last three works is based on the recognition of duality. Their action was to create the corridor between what we do and what we are, by *passing through* it.

From the finite repertory of human activities, the Open Theater selected those during which we are available to the unknown. The dance. The journey. The testimony. The dream. Like the dual themes of the plays, which are not considered suitable topics for conversation in the bourgeois world, these activities are seldom lived. We carry their shapes inside, and are full of their potential. But days are passed in conversation, argument, buying, selling, copying, arranging, ordering, submitting, compromising.

Within the activities are emblems; sounds, gestures, words or combinations of these selected by the actors as the essence of an action. Joe writes: "If an emblematic part of an action is played out, with the actor living *in* the action, there is a resonance beyond what there would be if the entire action were played out." The emblem connects actor and audience at this moment and connects the living and the dead through time. Maybe the only immortality is in the patterns the emblems recall. We die. The patterns persist. They alone give evidence of shared humanity. The emblem sets the pattern vibrating again in our space. Each of the Open Theater's last three works is centered on an

13

extended emblematic scene during which the actors spend the whole of their artistic energy putting their bodies visibly into the midst of change.

Recently the theater has become useless to the bourgeoisie. Broadway, off-Broadway, institutional theaters are floundering, their product lifeless, their audiences bored. The State has strayed so far from a notion of community that theater no longer makes sense within it. Yet the longing for community persists because the function of community is to be present as a totality during the times when the consciousness of individual members is fragmented by death, by joy, by grief, or pain or fear. Theater has community as its essential form. The audience is the uninitiate, the desperate people, the lost and vulnerable. Without an audience, so are the actors. As the two groups meet they are both made whole. In a culture where the dying are treated like objects that will soon be obsolete, *Terminal* restores death's rightful dignity. *Mutation Show* does the same for birth and education. And *Nightwalk* brings dreams back into the communal consciousness. The Open Theater gathered an audience around them at the moments when they felt most strongly community's lack. At such moments bourgeois realism is clearly useless. A boundary has been crossed. The location of the stage changes from the private living room into the public imagination. To unfold oneself before an audience. There is a wild generosity about anyone who can do this. All the Open Theater actors are beautiful in this way. They are raw with intensity.

Joe's parents were Russian immigrants who, he says, never showed a moment's tenderness towards each other. His father was an educated man. In Brooklyn he worked in a sweater factory. Joe has a defective heart. "When I was six they didn't know if I would live to be ten." His parents, needing one less mouth to feed, sent him to a home in Florida where for the first six months he lived alone in a room. If his parents had been middle class, I wonder, would rheumatic fever have been so damaging? Would he have been sick at all if the house was well-heated, the food more nutritious, doctors available? When his family moved to Des Moines, Iowa, for economic reasons, they were outcast because they are Jews. Joe is a pacifist. Not surprisingly, he has often been arrested for this view.

He has not been out of danger for one instant.

We look at the world, and we say, "What can I do?" And we answer, "Very little." And then some people, doing very little, just living their lives, come together and accomplish a great deal. Because one of them lives with death so intimately, they all make a play called *Terminal*. And suddenly they are in the midst of the transformations that will control their esthetic until they disband and will also dictate that final choice. And the rest of us look to them, as we are looking everywhere, for clues.

Terminal begins with an invocation: "We come among the dying to call upon the dead/Let them take my body/Let them use my tongue/ Let the dead come through/And let it begin with me." These words are spoken until their meaning is consumed by the rising energy of the dance. Then everyone is silent. They wait. Their bodies are limp without desire. They give their attention to the unknown. And now the dead come through. And the dance begins again. No words. There is only the reverberating sound of the sticks the actors carry. They pound on every surface. They fill the space up with the sound. Now the testimonies can begin.

The actors do not use emotional recall in order to present the testimonies. In fact, they could not. What in their past experience would amount to the sensation of speaking after death through another person's body? These testimonies present the essential Open Theater acting problem. In order to develop freely, the actor has to be rid of the limits of his or her emotional past. The constricting bourgeois fantasy that makes the past the sole determinant of the present severs us from our potential life and would by its very nature forbid *Terminal* from taking place. Abandonment, receptivity, repetition — in place of recall — make this experience possible. With these principles the Open Theater has reinvented acting for us. And more than this: by reinventing acting, they have redefined the possibilities for action within the world.

The testimonies are structured as confessions and accusations. They are filled with despair at the impenetrable barrier between perception and action. "I saw a child choking on air/What have I done?" demands Tina Shepard, become the Responsible One. And she cries out, "What was given me was impossible to work with." The judgments imagined by the dying and directed toward the audience echo this gap, "You saw, you saw, you can't say you didn't. The judgment of your life is your life."

All the while the repeated physical and vocal abandonment of the actors undercuts the deep despair of their words. The stage direction reads, "At the moment when the dead come through, everything is altered — ideas about life, attitudes toward death, rhythms, sounds and movements." During the frenzy of the dances on the graves of the dead the actors offer their bodies as corridors for the unknown. As they let themselves be taken over, these actors in a play about impermanence achieve a variation on the kind of immortality art makes possible. Through their work the dead appear to us.

15

The muscular connections made by the actors between the two worlds become far more profound than the initial rational perception of the separation between them.

> Thus, in a certain sense, the organic body can be regarded as the link between the will and the intellect; although properly speaking, the body is the will itself spatially exhibiting itself in the perception of the intellect.
>
> *Schopenhauer*

Paul Zimet's testimony in *Terminal* is different from the others; it establishes a category of speech specific to the Open Theater which is equivalent to the energy present in their bodies. In his Seeing speech, Paul, become Marie Leveau, a Creole sorceress, explains the sense of connection to all humanity that has defined the seers of every age. The means of its delivery — Paul gives up his voice to her — shows us something else the seers have known: self-realization comes after self-abandonment.

Terminal lessens none of the pain of individual extinction because, though it mediates between living and dying, the two worlds are in fact irreconcilable.

The union of the finite with the indefinable, of the single consciousness and the universal soul, is the problem posed by death. Every meditation on this theme, if it has merit, gives rise to a way of acting in this life.

Terminal is their most timeless work, and most tormented. *The Mutation Show* is a carnival piece, made in 1970 when the youthful counter-culture connected with the actors' own sense of possibility. It is their most linear work and the most consistently comic. The serious segments make it resonate, but they do not retard its movement. It progresses from the pain of past socialization procedures through the end of the nuclear family to the pleasure of liberated lives.

The members of the Mutants Gallery, introduced in the opening parade, have all selected a psychological "deformity" common among contemporary men and women: Ray Barry is The Man Who Hits Himself, Tom Lillard The Man Who Smiles, Paul Zimet The Petrified Man ("each day he moves less and less"). Tina Shepard as The Thinker who "thinks she thinks, but doesn't know what it is that she thinks" is woman in the midst of consciousness-raising. Jo Ann Schmidman, The Bird Lady who "wiggles and writhes, writhes and wiggles," is woman still acting out oppression. Shami Chaikin is The Sideshow Barker. She and Ellen Maddow, musician for this piece, provide the narrative links between scenes.

The carnival motif in *The Mutation Show* serves the same function as the dances on the graves of the dead in *Terminal*. It establishes a situation, comic this time, in which anything can happen. While the dances in *Terminal* were repeated actions of individual abandonment, the carnival sections in the *The Mutation Show* abandon history. They lead to a repetitive waltz that becomes a true wedding of opposites, the comic and serious modes are merged and history's pain forgotten through delight in present-day transformations.

The Mutants' opening parade is followed by the two consistently serious scenes in *The Mutation Show*. Both are introduced by Shami's brief narration and then occur without words. Kaspar Hauser spent the first 16 years of his life in a box. When he appeared in Nueremberg in 1826 he was unable to walk upright or to speak. Kamala and Omala grew up with a wolf pack. They were captured by hunters and taken to a Christian orphanage where they lived a few years. The events selected from both these stories allow for the increased complexity of Open Theater style. Once their vision was clearly formulated in the overall schema of *Terminal*, it began to shape and make distinctive each activity in which they invested energy.

Paul plays the Kaspar character. Ray, as his keeper, brutally pulls him from his box and puts him on his shoulders. They begin a wordless journey that is the visual working-out of a judgment in *Terminal*: "Did you sit on another's head or were you sat upon? Either way, you will never be free of the one who is above or he who is below."

Ray walks. Paul slumps around his neck. Ray walks. He adjusts Paul's weight. Paul begins to notice things around him. He begins to see, and as he begins to see his body takes on a will of its own. His weight shifts. He climbs up Ray's shoulders. He stretches out from Ray's waist. He becomes a burden. Ray rips him from his shoulders and leaves him terrified at the top of a hill. Paul produces a high-pitched scream. For the prisoner there is a special anguish at the moment of separation.

Part of Kaspar Hauser's diary tells how he cursed his freedom until one day he fell down and saw the stars and from that minute began to curse his keeper for hiding him from such magnificence. Paul's and Ray's journey was developed from this section. Joe says that all the questions Kaspar asked received simple answers until he saw the sky and asked how far away the stars are. With his first unanswerable question, he was truly born. Once determined, this interpretation of the diary disappeared into the shape of the journey. Paul's and Ray's movements might mean any of a dozen things. Their journey has become a physical relation between bodies, the outlines of which are so sharp they call up numerous psychic relations between masters and slaves, all sorts of theoretical ones between intellect and experience. In the real sense that makes it art, Paul's and Ray's journey has no meaning outside itself. Or, to say it another way, it receives every meaning within itself. It is understanding in its clearest form, present without explanation.

Now Tina and Jo Ann are rescued from the wolf pack. Jo Ann is violently lassoed. Tina is artfully seduced by a hunter, Tom Lillard, who begins to breath in her rhythm. She relaxes and allows him to approach. For a moment they breathe together, side by side. For one moment, they are related. Then Tom swings his rope over Tina and tightens it around her diaphragm. She jumps and all her breath leaves her.

"Breathing," Joe said one day in a workshop, "is the key to internal movement. Through its rhythm what we know as experience is expressed." It's possible for Tom to breathe with Tina only for a while. If they breathed together for a longer time it would mean that Tom had given up the hunter's sensibility. The horror of this capture is intensified by focusing on the moment when it could have been otherwise.

It's not just their superb technique, or that they came upon an interesting event, or even the two in combination, that allows such richness at each instant. There is nothing about either their breathing techniques or the story of the capture of the wild child that could not be learned or copied. But put between them the *idea* that breath reveals the true nature of experience, and the scene lives far in excess of its parts. The authentic connection between theater techniques and dramatic subjects is an idea of the world that transforms them both.

Look at what has happened to the activities themselves. They have become elemental, sensual, physical. In the realistic theater, and even in the periods before it, *breathing* or *seeing* do not exist as activities on which the audience is focused. The time is taken up by *confessing, shaming, quarreling, judging, persuading, seducing*. . . . The Open Theater found many of its central activities in physical processes instead of taking them from the more abstract level of human intention. Doing this, they changed the concept of life that theater activity presents. People are no longer to be defined according to what they achieve but by the energy with which they participate in sustaining life.

As activity was redefined, words were necessarily displaced. But I wonder if this will always be so, or if we are not already near that future state when *seeing, breathing, dancing* will resonate enough through the minds of people that passions will begin to be discussed in terms of them, and writers will reenter the theater to do it.

The Mutants repeat their opening parade, but it has been changed in its turn through insertion of comic emblems that refer back to the preceding serious sections. Shami carries Ray. Jo Ann masturbates on the rope once used to restrain her. Tina and Paul stage a mock struggle. Here is the opening sentence of Marx's *Eighteenth Brumaire*: "Hegel remarks somewhere that all facts and personages of great importance in world history occur, as it were, twice. He forgot to add: the first time as tragedy, the second as farce." Farce is a moment in any move toward liberation because it undoes alienation, even if wrongheadedly. Farce tends toward display, a wholly self-involved activity during which the character lives out his or her project, thereby closing the gap between desire and experience. But what the comic character wants is in some way ridiculous; there is something ignoble in the project itself. So its temporary achievement opens our perception to the gap bteween the character's realized egocentricity and the real work of feeling oneself at home in the world.

Ray Barry comes out of the box covered with a gelatinous mixture of his excretions. He speaks a Seeing speech. Like Paul's journey, it is about the birth of self-consciousness, and it ends with *The Mutation Show*'s recurring theme: "I don't know if this happened to me or to someone else but I know it happened." Tina is pulled upright and taught to walk in shoes. But she might be one of the side-show attractions so quickly is the pain of her steps obscured by the din of a backstage jam session on kazoo, block, slide whistle, cigar-box fiddle, and Ellen Maddow's accordion. The symphonic chaos introduces the contemporary rite of socialization, the wedding that perpetuates the nuclear family. The Mutants parade in pairs, displaying the deformities of the organism we call the couple. They come down the aisle like toy dolls, mechanical people. Jo Ann pants at her husband's side. Tina is passed uncomprehending from father to husband.

Ellen begins the "Anniversary Waltz," and the Mutants enter into a stylized ¾ step. "The bride is now dancing with the groom. . . The bride is now dancing with the mother of the groom. . . The mother of the groom is now dancing with the mayor." Her description continues, and the Mutants continue their repetitive waltz steps. "The cow is now dancing with the butcher," Ellen says. Shami and Tina kiss. A heterosexual couple and woman masturbating climax simultaneously and roll joyfully across the stage. The Mutants stop. They isolate the ¾ rhythm in a twitching finger, Adam's apple, or chest muscle. "The oil men are now dancing with the generals." The Mutants find a second wind. They take up the dance with renewed vigor. Ray does extraordinary leaps across the stage. "The dead are now dancing with the newborn." The wedding of family and state has been undone and a nonhierarchical wedding of opposites effected.

The dances in *Terminal* relied upon abandonment. The wedding dance of *The Mutation Show* discovers how repetition relates to change. You have a movement and you repeat it to the limits of endurance, and suddenly you get a second wind. The kinetic principles have not been changed, but the new energy increases the possibility of self-expression. By pushing ourselves harder and harder against the boundaries, we come to sense where the structure is weakest and where it might be broken through. Repetition is the mode of the field slave, wife, or assembly-line worker. It makes everybody very weary, but it also makes a way.

After the wedding dance the performers drop their masks and offer themselves and their own transformations as further proof of what their play has been about. They stand across the stage holding pictures of themselves before they joined the Open Theater. Tom was a marine. Shami wore a synthetic scarf and smile. Paul was stuffed into a suit and tie. Tina had a tight page-boy. Ellen recites facts about their height and weight, their families, and their previous lives: "Tina Shepard's Uncle John is a federal judge." "In the sixth grade Paul Zimet won the American Legion Citizenship Award."

To end, the Mutants give testimony. They come through the curtain singly, repeating variations on recurrent Open Theater emblems. Tom runs in place recalling the "runner who never gets started" from the world of the dying in *Terminal*. Shami breathes heavily and makes a consonant sound at the front of her mouth, but she cannot form a single word. Ray hits himself, but then retards this motion, recalling the way his hands framed his face when he came out of the box and saw light. Jo Ann is still The Bird Lady, yet she also says the thematic sentence: "I don't know if this happened to me or to someone else but I know it happened."

Perhaps Paul's testimony comes the closest to suggesting the reason for their work: "I do it the way I was taught it. I see it the way it was shown to me." During the Open Theater's final performances in New York, which coincided with the fascist takeover of Chile and the resumption of war in the Middle East, Joe would often repeat, "I really do believe we see it the way it is shown to us. And if we could see it in a different way. . . ." I don't remember that he ever finished the sentence. But he didn't need to — the work makes the thought clear this far. And he couldn't — because there we were in the fall of 1973 staring at events whose horrors are so far impervious to the force of this vision.

When the Open Theater started in 1963, the actors were most in need of venting their feelings of alienation. They produced social satires on anti-war themes such as *Sunday Morning* and *Eating the Corpse* and

their bitter denunciation of commodity culture, *America Hurrah!* In
The Serpent they found they could surpass alienation by concentrating
on questions they shared about guilt and choice. With *Terminal* and
The Mutation Show they gave their shared experience a transformational
shape. But there was one more work to do.

Since 1968 the interior opposition between Presence and Absence
has solidified into a gross external and paralysing opposition between
Us and Them. What was only dimly perceived before 1968 has become
practically possible. The movement is no longer a fad, and what it has
lost in visibility it has made up for in seriousness and depth. Yet one
can feel only despair about national politics and economics, sexism and
racism. And the people are so traumatized by front-line battle in the
class war that they seem to be as sexist and racist as the government.
Every one of us is a moral amputee. But those who know this and concentrate on how it could be otherwise are full of great energy and a real
sense of well-being unmatched in any other segment of United States
society. Inside the movement, we know we are nurturing new lives.

The opposing possibilities that were the subjects of psychoanalytic,
linguistic, and political theories provided the impetus for the Open
Theater. Now they have become actual. We are alive in a world of
drastic contrast. The Open Theater and Standard Oil both work here,
but on what grounds could they communicate? *Nightwalk* addresses
the schizophrenia within the human race.

It is their virtuoso work, created at the limits of ability where daring
and control establish perfect tension. *The Mutation Show* hurtled toward
this edge. *Terminal* reached it repeatedly through incredible abandonment. In contrast, *Nightwalk*'s achievement appears effortless. The
piece is inexhaustibly spacious. It neither contains the mystery nor
lets it go but wanders around within it.

I saw an open rehearsal of *Nightwalk* during which Joe spent the
entire time eliminating the music, which was then quite complex. When
Nightwalk opened in New York the actors sometimes played two small
drums by dropping rubber balls on top of them, and there was a short
flute solo that filled your head with its beauty. Otherwise, mostly silence. Yet there is a rhythm to this work that demands complete attention. Not one second in it is arbitrary. The space is always filled yet
fluid. The grace of the paths of the rough wood and metal carts the
characters are stuck to is as real as the ferocity with which the characters
are portrayed.

Ellen and Ralph Lee, Ray, Shami, Jo Ann and Tom simper and guffaw, bellow and screech. The men are mainly engaged in boasting. The
women are ingratiating. When the characters move off the carts they do

21

it slowly and laboriously. They are overstuffed with the fruits of capital. Their bodies are inexpressive, their faces overactive, their words a garbled string of familiar platitudes. With their eyes they see nothing.

Yet if anywhere within these mutilated beings there exists a collective wish for wholeness, then *Nightwalk* images its fulfillment. Tina and Paul, as Creature and Traveler, are approaching androgyny. Tina: instinct — nonverbal, alert, inquisitive, daring, active. Paul: reason — watchful, contemplative, capable. "You are the other part of me," he tells her. In days when physical love is less and less possible because we no longer tolerate, yet do not know how to overcome, genital tyranny, Tina and Paul make love to each other with their lives. They form a tender dialectic transcending individual potential. They become a model for community.

Tina and Paul prepare for their journey through the world as it is known to us. He takes the opening minutes to carefully slice an apple, their ration for the tour. She explores the space. No words. No sounds until, surprised by the crash of a platform she has unwittingly upset, she utters the glottal flutter that (along with a squawk and a hiss) is her only vocal means of communication. She eats the apple peel and stops. Her silver eyes beam energy at the audience. She holds us still. Time is arrested by her intensity.

For much of *Nightwalk*, Tina and Paul hold hands. The circle is completed by the metal frame under which they walk and to which they are joined. Paul's slow steady steps are punctuated by the low, sharp drum roll; Tina's lateral hops jingle the silver bells around her ankles. The people of the world sweep past these two. The carts come silently on rubber wheels. Their motion is dreamlike, but the people rooted there are wholly familiar. Ray and Tom present the Men's World. They exchange off-color stories, make dirty sounds, guffaw. Their faces are contorted, their bodies immobilized by a macho pose. Jo Ann and Ellen slump together coyly, the Women's World. Through their giggles we hear them comparing cock sizes. Two separate ways. One gentle and aware. The other closed and harping. But *Nightwalk* would be only a vindictive work if limited to this initial perception. Once the disparity has been established, a passage between the worlds must be suggested. What else is worth having in art right now except such patterns for transcendence?

The people appear crowded together on one cart. They are drafting an Indictment to God, charging him with the crime of absence. This is the scene that links the audience to the people. Aside from their ugliness, their pessimism is also recognizable; one sees its visage all the time on city streets. The helmets and goggles the actors have put on reproduce this paralytic stare.

The Indictment scene is a departure from Open Theater style. The mode of delivery is only an appendage; its essence is contained within the words. The usual judgment schema has three parts: the charge, the questioning, which allows for presentation of the evidence, and the sentencing. Sometime during presentation of the evidence a shift occurs that makes a sentence possible. The dramatic purpose of judging scenes is usually to redefine the nature of justice. In the Indictment scene the shift that occurs also calls into question the validity of judging by showing how much the people who judge are diminished by the activity of judging. To sentence God for being absent is simultaneously to recognize and to banish the potential grace within oneself. The Indictment is the opposite of Genesis: it creates the void. "You are the absence I have lived with always." But it also creates the longing that the void be filled and so gives urgency to *Nightwalk*'s work.

At night, Freud tells us, we dream through all our wishes. What a curious formulation, really: that dreams are fulfilled only during sleep and that their function is to let the sleep continue.

The Sleep scene is *Nightwalk*'s most emblematic part. The people on the carts are breathing slowly and steadily. They are wrapped around each other in beautiful combinations. In their dream state they recall the limits of their waking lives. Tom and Shami (Boss and Girl Friend from the Boss's Supper scene) dream through their lover's quarrel. Shami hints at her hysteria. Then, as though it were not a part of her, one arm reaches up and remains aching in air. Mute testimony. Ray has a nightmare about his job, but he also enjoys an instant of grace. His body recalls the posture of the stately Heron, an Open Theater emblem for Eden since Paul created it in *The Serpent*.

The Sleep scene compares to the wedding dance from *The Mutation Show* and the calling up of the dead in *Terminal*, but it lacks their insistent energy. It has a quieter kind of beauty. The actors' energies are reactive — rather than initiating events they are adjusting to the impact of events that have happened. What the uses of reactive scenes are is still mysterious. Yet clearly the restraints imposed by periods of reaction can sometimes allow for freedom. In tragedy reactive speeches have traditionally occurred the moment after a central character hears the dreaded news. Before another action can be taken the character's psychic structure must stretch to accommodate the seriousness of past events. During this pause one's life is in review, and the momentum of domination/submission might become undone. But in order for this

23

structural change to occur, another possible world view would have to enter consciousness along with description of the catastrophic news.

The dream conceit in *Nightwalk* allows for exactly this. Paul and Tina wander around the Sleep scene. They are being dreamt. The previous day's occurrences, represented by the specific emblematic gestures of the actors, are only the vehicles by means of which repressed desires surface. Paul's and Tina's presence becomes the crucial emblem for an entirely other way of being in the world. They envision exactly the non-authoritarian, androgynous possibility that Freud's position in middle-class, anti-Semitic Austria demanded he repress.

After the Sleep scene all is changed; *Nightwalk* enters fully the motion of transcendence. The comic moments which before had been concerned with satirizing the bourgeoisie now acquire luster. Their content may be less sophisticated, but their execution is more nearly classic, their intentions more exuberant. Paul and Tina lose one another. To get back together they engage in a perfectly timed chase sequence around the backdrop curtains. When they finally meet face-to-face and recognize each other, their joy is so complete they begin to dance. The circular patterns of the chase, like a sped-up version of the paths followed by the carts, are replaced by the vertical leaps of their dance. All this movement comes directly after the spacious quietude of the Sleep scene. *Nightwalk*'s changing rhythms make a feast.

Tina jumps into Paul's arms. Her legs wrap around his waist. She is close to his chest when he begins to walk. They are a happily inverted version of Paul's and Ray's journey from *The Mutation Show*. Paul turns a Navajo chant into a particularly lovely Seeing speech: "In beauty I walk/ With beauty before me I walk/With beauty above and about me I walk." One wonders if pacifism is possible until one sees such a perfect witness to it.

Suddenly *Nightwalk* breaks into a display of popular culture. The carts sweep past in the sensational rhythms of television spectaculars. Posing performers croon out fantasies: "My Defenses Are Down," "Everytime We Say Goodbye," "I'm in the Mood for Love." Jo Ann, dressed in a flowing chiffon gown, holding a plastic rose, is placed onstage like a plastic mannequin. She sings a Christian hymn in torch song style: "And the joys we share as we tarry there/None other has ever known." Ray, dressed like a tramp, is rushed onto the stage. He climbs off his cart and begins molesting Jo Ann. He grabs her hand hand and bumps it up and down against his groin. He crawls under her skirt, turning his back to us to show a bare ass hanging out between a slit in his pants. In this position, Ray and Jo Ann appear as a single

24

unfeeling body: they are the grotesque opposite of the fluid androgynous shapes achieved by Paul and Tina. Now he picks her up and tips her upside down to get a better taste. Jo Ann does not miss one note in her hymn. The two activities, rape and devotion, proceed simultaneously, and through their combination, *Nightwalk* passes beyond satire to blasphemy, humor that both mocks and penetrates the sacred social hierarchy.

Tina has entered midway in this scene to join in the sensual play. She rubs against Ray and Jo Ann, leans over to sniff his ass, purrs with satisfaction. Ray, sensing only interference, throws her out. Then, finished with Jo Ann, he does a brief jig, blows his plastic whistle, shows us his behind once more, and leaves "flamboyantly." Tina also engages in a moment of fully self-absorbed satisfaction. She leaves Paul, stands alone in the frame and with great delight mimics expressions she has learned from the people of the world: "We're having a wonderful time." "We've taken a lot of pictures." "Filthy child-molesting faggots·. . . in their commie, pinko parked cars. . . ." Ray and Tina have both entered into display. A sought, but inappropriate, project has been realized by each of them.

The light dims. Some chimes. Ray transformed into the Heron appears on the stage. Creature and Heron approach one another. Two beautiful beings at home in this twilight night. Suddenly they begin to fight. Tina wounds Ray deeply. They screech. Two beautiful beings in combat. Joe says this scene shows the physical relationships possible between living beings: they can turn away from one another, make loving contact, or fight. The Creature and the Heron do all three in turn. Creature and Heron play this scene, Joe says, because with human characters one would want a psychological explanation for the fighting. The Battle scene is meant as an example, a proposition simply. Here is the theater as a lecture hall, but the problem is posed with exquisite physicality.

Yet no matter what the intention of the ensemble, the audience views the battle as a continuation of the action. In this context it becomes a painful thing. In *Nightwalk* Paul teaches Tina and Tina teaches Ray. But the Creature is not easy with the Heron and neither is the Traveler easy with the Creature. He makes no attempt to keep her from from display or combat. He sits quietly to the side and does not interfere until the Heron lies screaming on the ground. The exemplary person is not someone who lessens your pain, or who is not critical, or who is easy to endure. The exemplary person is the one who demands that you know yourself.

The Traveler reclaims the Creature, and when they are secure within the frame again he delivers a speech containing emblems from the entire piece but organizing none of them. Shami spins by, banging a tambourine. And Ray is pushed out to ask *Nightwalk*'s essential question: "There was himself and herself and herself and himself/and between us. . ." With his right hand he makes a serpent-like motion that suggests simultaneously our separateness and our connecting energies. What's between us is only what we put there. There is no natural law for the separations we have created. Paul and Tina are witness to this potentiality. So is Ray, perhaps even more instructively, because without him *Nightwalk* would contain two irreconcilable experiences. While working on this piece Ray developed into so supple an actor that he is able to provide the link between the two worlds. He passes from the boasting of the Men's World to the display of the Clowns' World to the self-realization of the Heron. His individual action distinguishes a pattern that has been present in the company's work since *Terminal*. And Tina's movement from the Creature's androgynous existence to her display of bourgeois slogans to her initiation of the fight repeats this pattern backwards to leave its outlines more clearly in our memory.

Display is already a disruption of the logic of domination; it replaces the capitalists' cruel fragmentation of time with a delight in the present moment. We might say display was the first disruption practised by the Open Theater, because the moment it occurs acting turns from representation to presentation.

But display is a child's game, a momentary joy tolerated by a world guaranteed to mutilate, destroy, or package it. It is the avant-garde theater. Self-realization is adult, a way of being in the world established within oneself, which becomes a model for the world as it might be. Self-realization is radical because it reclaims work from the marketplace, anarchist because it follows the creative order inherent in human nature, nonviolent and androgynous because it admits no hierarchy nor any separations based on role.

What turns display into self-realization? The same qualities that have so distinguished the work of the Open Theater. Repetition, attention, abandonment, receptivity — combined with the artist's obligation to transform our vision of the world.

Have the Open Theater actors changed individually doing this work? I didn't know them as friends in the early years. I don't know them well now. I finally met everyone in the company during their last five weeks in New York before the cross-country tour that would end their livelihood and their work together. They are all intelligent, talented, warm people who were then under enormous pressure. They were faced with becoming commercial actors again. A true community would never make a formal decision to disband. The nature of their final choice defines the limits of their life together.

How have they changed as actors? Here the information is all public and also revealing. *Terminal* is a dazzling metaphysical feat; it turns actors into shamans come before the community to reveal the unknown. Yet the activities within some of its scenes now appear quite simple. During the Initiation Ray hits Paul on the head until Paul learns to produce only those answers that please his master. Compare this activity to Paul's and Ray's journey or the animal pack in *The Mutation Show*. These scenes also explain the mechanisms of domination, but they are performed with an energy and subtle physicality that turn them equally into metaphors for liberation. The carts in *Nightwalk* make a bitter comment on the mental immobility of the bourgeoisie. At the same time the rhythms of their passage around the space provide much of the beauty of the piece. We might understand the intricacy of Open Theater technique as the permeation of structural dualities into the separate segments of each work. Similarly, self-realization is human potential moved from the abstract realm of thought to the concrete realm of experience. Self-realization becomes possible as a theater activity only insofar as the actors have felt it in their own lives.

Perhaps Shami's singing of the Jewish prayer for the dead in *Terminal* is the first solo moment of self-abandonment reached by any of the four actors who were with the company the longest. The song takes us beyond character and its attendant neuroses to the awful impersonality of grief. "The song fills the woman. It uses her voice to sing itself." The stage direction, written after the fact, is an accurate description of what happened. Shami's understanding is seldom expressed verbally, but since *Terminal* the authority of her presence has always been manifest. In *The Mutation Show* she is The Barker — the person who announces the scenes and sets the rhythm of their sequence. In *Nightwalk* her simple statements — "Now I'm standing up," "Now I'm turning and saying these words" — and her matching actions are in vivid contrast to the confusion of the bourgeoisie. She does not come into direct contact with the Creature or the Traveler, but she circles around them like a moon. At the end of the piece she spins by while playing a tambourine, and the energy she beams at the audience is equivalent to the Creature's.

Paul's and Tina's perception of nonsexist relationships which allows them to imagine the Traveler and the Creature is inseparable from their ability to act them. Perhaps it is not accidental that while they were married to each other the activities they chose were other than self-realization. Tina's Responsible One speech in *Terminal* (which she did

27

not originate, but inherited from a former member of the company) is based on confession and self-accusation, two activities immediately recognizable to women existing within the nuclear family. In *The Mutation Show* her attempted confession during the testimonies, "I swear to tell the whole truth. . ." is halted by the beginnings of self-consciousness, "This is not my voice." In *Nightwalk* she uses words only when she lapses from self-realization back into display. At all other moments she holds us not by revealing the conflicts within herself but in awe at the contrast between her intensity and our own.

Ray's Executed Man speech in *Terminal* is composed of confession, accusation, and storytelling activities. Its theme is the perversion of the imagination. He extols the murderous images inside us all: "Everything I imagine is part of me." In *The Mutation Show* he has a Seeing speech. The activities are storytelling and beginning self-consciousness. The words detail the distance between people but end with the sentence that asserts our unity: "I don't know if this happened to me or to someone else but I know it happened." In *Nightwalk* seeing is transformed into imagining. The activities are description and self-realization. Separations are overcome by an effort of the imagination: "The ship cuts me off from the house. The house from the fish. I'm inside that fish." The possibility suggested in the speech is realized in the play. Ray alone has access to both worlds; his increased imagination as an actor allows him this.

Paul's changes while with this company have been less spectacular than Ray's or Tina's, but his presence has been no less profound. Paul's speeches and his gestures show us the limits the Open Theater left us facing. Amid the sadness of *The Serpent* Paul found the Heron that was to be their lasting emblem of Eden. He delivered their first Seeing speech in *Terminal* and turned that verbal expression of new consciousness into the physical journey from the box in *The Mutation Show*, thus beginning Open Theater concentration on self-realization. In *Nightwalk* he let the power of the others dominate, but his dance with Tina and his chant have the serene courage of exemplary acts.

Before they even began to work together and until they disbanded, they thought that language had betrayed us, that words are what we render up to Mammon and that he drones them back at us as commercials. So they concentrated on their bodies and their voices and reached a range of sound and movement that refuted every easy, marketable meaning. Choosing this way of working as perhaps their most consistent means of protest, they revealed simultaneously a tendency to undercut, fragment, contrast, and a refusal to compare. It was part of the nature of their theater, this concern to expose one dogmatic way of thinking and at the same time not to replace it with another. The Elizabethan dramatists, trying to support a fading hierarchy, tended toward grand finales, scenes of magnificent summation. The Open Theater ends its last three works with the actors' simple presence in the space, breathing (*The Mutation Show*) or walking (*Nightwalk*) or (*Terminal*) crawling on their bellies, at once the worms that devour the bodies of the dead and the children in the birth canal.

Paul's last speech in *Nightwalk* is as close as they came to summation. Its content and his manner of delivery seek correspondence with their physical ability to extend the edge before retreat. The speech is a collectively arrived at composite of sentences from previous parts of the piece, lines from poems by Ted Hughes and Wallace Stevens, words written for it by Sam Shepard. Its three sections explore and undercut philosophical, physical, and existential limits.

Paul invests this pastiche with energy but not with a distinctive shape. He runs through it like a scale, filling each line with new emotion until what remains in one's head is the richness of his voice. The lines have tonal but not metaphoric life. The Open Theater's work stopped here, where physical presence must go back again to understanding to find the further evolutions of its shape.

I began by saying the Open Theater has made a great esthetic and ethical statement. I will end by suggesting that partly because of their work the two are no longer separate in our minds. If esthetics is the study of what is beautiful and ethics is knowledge of the good, then we have seen their reconciliation in these three works. Oppositions have given them their structure, contrasts their dynamic, and transformation the active vision necessary to art. In other ages other ethical questions have logically occupied the minds of men and women but we live under a state that is murdering all the people in the world, what else can we concentrate on but change. And how else can we concentrate on change except by posing the inner and the outer, presence and absence, community and patriarchy, ourselves and the other, and then discovering every possible corridor between them. These dualities contain the structure of revolution; they form theses and antitheses of the dialectic. And they contain an evolving equilibrium which provides the space to act out the grace that lives inside us all.

Karen Malpede
New York City
December 18, 1973

29

Notes on Acting Time and Repetition

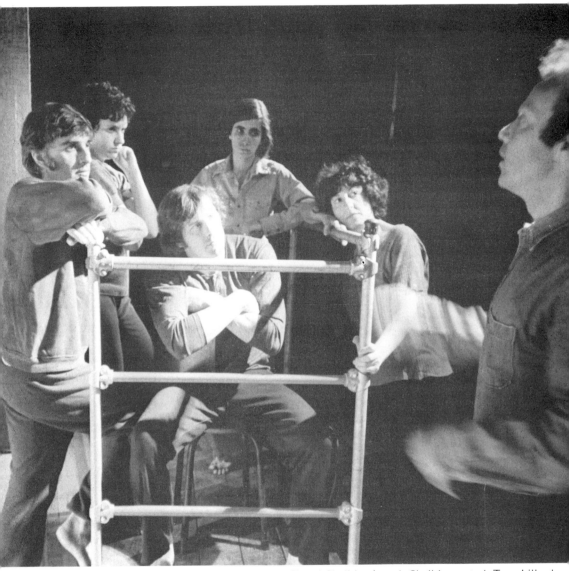

Ralph Lee, Ellen Maddow, Jo Ann Schmidman, Shami Chaikin, Joseph Chaikin; seated, Tom Lillard.

Photo: Inge Morath

32

The attempts to video tape or film the Open Theater works have all failed to transmit any part of the essential experience, which is the vibrating breathing actor, breathing in the breathing universe. The light of the eyes. The conscious body of the actor moving in the given space. The particular voice creating a living contact with the audience.

The most fundamental element of theater is "presence." For the actor to give form to the changing present, he or she must first understand that time is experienced in many diverse ways. His or her own usual cultural experience of time is only one form, rather than a fixed truth.

One fundamental difference between a person and a photograph of a person is the person is changing in time and the photograph is frozen. It is from this distinction that the stage actor makes choices.

In acting schools, while learning stage behavior, the young actor is also learning to interpret experience. Within the technique of acting is often a way of seeing. Later the actors' interpretation of experience becomes that of the audience.

Most acting exercises are practices that are used to develop something other than the exercise itself. What therefore remains insufficiently exercised in many workshop situations is the doing of the act itself – that of performing in the present – the act being itself. The developed actor is not practising in one moment what surprise he or she will do in the next. The action is not a reference to another action unplayed, but is itself. The actor is not making divisions between him or herself and the sum-self of the audience. The actor is working in a kind of third person present tense.

We are always in relation to time and to duration since once we become awake to them it is clear that every idea, every feeling, every volition is undergoing change at every moment.

Societies have unstated attitudes toward actual-time and eternal-time which are expressed in stories and symbols. The time stories that each society has as myth derive from and in turn recommend how people within that society regard their life-time.

In the capitalist world people often conceive of the present as something which is to happen later — as though the present is located in an anticipated (memory of the) future. The present time, when life begins, is still to come. Mostly we try to deal with time as an amount — time as a quantity that gets used up as we live, like a slow meal that you eat until it is gone.

Whenever we are not in a time flow, waiting is what we do with our life. I think it's fair to say that the main activity of most people, most of the time, is waiting. In the activity of waiting, a person is only partly present in what is taking place and is not even conscious that he or she is in service to waiting. On the one hand we live as though our life span were going to be 1000 years, so it doesn't really matter what we do for the first 100. And on the other there is the urgent requirement to appropriate time before someone else does.

Memory and habit move in on the present, as the present. The past cannot be controlled. It is the unchosen part of the present and is liberated only through a full assimilation of its having actually taken place.

We cannot hold time. We can only be in or out of its movement. To be out of time is not actually to be out of it but only out of synchronization between awareness and rhythm.

Moving with the present is taking an initiative in harmony with time. Rather than retreating from the moment, it is to embody the moment. If we let the present in, psychic pressure is generally relieved, since psychic pressure comes mostly from investing in the imagined possible outcome of what hasn't happened yet.

In this age, we have too definitely divided the mind from the body and the visceral. Life experience plays through us, if we let it. As actors, as artists, we are vessels through which ideas come in the form of feelings — and feelings in the form of ideas.

If an actor convincingly plays a character who is very different from him or herself, what are we to say of him or her? Is he or she really like that? Or: is he or she a very convincing simulator? Or: are there infinite choices of acts and infinite numbers of faces in one actor-person? Where does the actor draw from in him or herself to play a role on stage very

Paul Zimet, Tina Shepard, Joseph Chaikin

Photo: Inge Morath

unlike his or her life role? And where is this energy all the rest of the time? The largest questions dealing with acting in the theater also deal with acting in life. An actor-person who sees life as being completely contained within the describable situations which he or she moves in and out of and which move in and around him or her is necessarily an actor in the service of a limited idea. Thus the psychological actor sees the space of a house as the full scope and vastness of experience, and when he or she inadvertently looks up and sees the sky he or she sees it as nothing more than a covering for the house.

35

But there are poets and artists who can reflect extreme conditions. The more developed artist reflects conditions unmediated by sympathy or conscience. Would we indict the messenger for the crimes he or she reports? Any theme that inspires the artist is potentially useful. It is not the responsibility of art to serve any politics or psychology or philosophy. The realm of art is inspiration, and inspiration cannot be policed even by noble motives.

It is the double responsibility of art to be faithful to the subtle promptings of intuition — and to the audience. The one requires the artist to surrender to intuition and the other to bring about conscious form and clarity.

The artist who employs his or her art as a means of recruiting converts to any particular issue — whether political, religious, or psychological — has gotten caught up in the world of salesmanship.

The significant political choices are involved in the artist's relationships to his or her collaborators, to the audience, and to commerce.

Opinions mean little. Rhetoric means little now. Whether a group chooses to work with political or nonpolitical issues has nothing to do with its real political existence — the directly political questions that face every theater have to do with money and the coexistence between members of a company, between the company and the audience, and between the company and management. Essentially the political questions that face a theater are the same as those that face any individual.

The theme of the play may be anything from a love story to a nightmare. The point is that when the direct, daily life problems of a company are explored noncoercively, the company's political commitment is clear no matter what the theme of the play. There are sounds and rhythms that may lead to social alienation just as, say, architecture and education may. So finding the right words and themes for a theater piece is only part of the work; the formal elements of presentation — such as sound and rhythm — have social effects too.

Growing older is a process not confined to anyone. The infant grows older in what seems to be a more rapid pace. The adult grows older in what seems to be a more gradual pace. But everyone grows older in the same direction.

The main thing in growing older is how repetition affects us.

Joseph Chaikin

Photo: Mary Ellen Mark

We walk in and out of more doors each month. As we grow older we
live through more nights of dreaming uninterpretable dreams. We make
love more times. We endure more outrage. We witness more of what
seems meaningless. We discover ourselves caught in a new trap in an
old way.

The first time someone makes love is different from the fiftieth. The
first time someone wants to kill someone and doesn't is different from
the tenth. The first cognizance of the setting sun and the countless
galaxies is different from the eightieth. The first tragic personal loss
is different from subsequent ones.

Repetition is the essential difference in growing older. For some
it deepens and for others it hollows out experience.

Joseph Chaikin
New York City
October 16, 1973

A Note on the Texts

The text of *Terminal* printed here represents the final evolution of the piece as it
was being performed by the company during their final tour. A different version of
Terminal is published in *Scripts 1*, November 1971.

 The Mutation Show and *Nightwalk* have
never existed in traditional script form.
Each piece is the collective work of these
actors and several writers. Only the words
spoken by the actors are printed here.
No attempt has been made to include stage
directions, which at best would provide in-
accurate hints of what actually happened
during performance.

Terminal

TERMINAL

text by
SUSAN YANKOWITZ

co-directed by
JOSEPH CHAIKIN and ROBERTA SKLAR

The Ensemble:
   Raymond Barry
   Shami Chaikin
   Tom Lillard
   Jo Ann Schmidman
   Tina Shepard
   Paul Zimet

Musician:
   Ellen Maddow

Administrative director:
   John Stoltenberg

Production manager:
   Michael Bartuccio

Costumes:
   Gwen Fabricant

Lighting designed by:
   Arden Fingerhut

Administrative assistant:
   Patricia Berman

Production director:
   Stephen Rich

In a collective work there are
stages equal in significance to the
performance state. When the En-
semble begins to prepare directly
for the performing stage, it relies
entirely on the initial investigations.
We would like to acknowledge the
following people for their partici-
pation in the development of
TERMINAL:
Dick Peaslee and Stanley Walden,
composers; Marc Kaminsky, Nancy
Martin and Sam Shepard, writers;
Joyce Aaron, James Barbosa,
Brenda Dixon, Ron Faber, Sharon
Gans, Jayne Haynes, Ralph Lee,
Peter Maloney, Muriel Miguel,
Mark Samuels, Ellen Schindler,
Barbara Vann, Lee Worley, actors;
and Marianne de Pury, Dale Whitt,
Joseph Campbell, Mossa Bildner,
Kesang-tomma, Ronald Laing,
and Muir Weisinger.

The Sequence

Style and Structure

The style of the piece is presentational.

It is constructed of general sections within which are a series of fragments.

Each fragment is a self-contained entity that relates to the others and to the whole through juxtapositions and associations.

Every section and fragment is introduced by a title. A single actor, or several, may perform this function during the course of the play.

Blackouts are used to define the beginning and end of major sections. These blackouts not only delineate distinct thematic areas, but also provide a stylistic counterpart to the cycle of life and death, presence and absence.

The movement from fragment to fragment shifts the piece back and forth through various levels of experience.

41

The Actors and the Space

The actors are always present.

When an actor is not directly engaged in the events onstage, he moves into a defined area around the periphery.

This space may be considered an onstage/offstage area in which the actor rests, prepares, changes costume, waits.

From this periphery an actor enters the acting area to join in an action. The line between the onstage and offstage area may be crossed.

There is only one space in which the actors are always visible.

Properties and Lights

Like the actors, all theatrical props and materials are visible.

Lights are hung in plain view of the audience.

Nothing is hidden or disguised, but everything can be transformed.

A pallet is a bed when placed horizontally on the floor. When upright, it is a wall.

A rack is a structure for hanging clothes. It is also an instrument of torture.

Lights may be used as spotlights or instruments of interrogation; they may be fixed overhead or held by the actors.

All objects are real objects. And what is constructed for the piece is obviously makeshift.

Everything is part of the theatrical world and derives its functions from the needs of that world.

The Roles

All roles are multiple and interchangeable.

The living are also the dying; the dying are potentially the dead. And the dead will become living matter.

The dying are close to death and sensitive to spiritual forces. Their heightened awareness makes possible their possession by the dead.

The Team supervise the institutions of life: they are the hospital attendants, the wardens, the embalmers. They may be portrayed by one person or by many, but they, too, are the dying.

The Music

Music is used in its broadest definition: it is pure sound and rhythm.

Some music is simply an extension of the human voice. The actors become instruments; they find and produce sounds that communicate emotions and experiences outside the usual range of human expression.

Some music is an extension of the human body. Hands and feet become instruments for eliciting music from surfaces — floor, walls, beds.

Language becomes incantation and incantation becomes music. Words dissolve into fragments and sounds.

Repetition of lines, sounds, and gestures recur as a means of suggesting associations between seemingly unrelated passages and of evoking resonances that enrich meaning.

When conventional instruments are used, they are always simple — harmonicas, tambourines, drums, sticks.

The Costumes

The piece is concerned with death and therefore with the body.

As a part of nature, the body must be revealed by the costume. As a part of society, it must be concealed.

In our production, simple white garments are worn by the actors. Each differs from the others in cut and style, but together they create an over-all impression of uniformity.

The costumes evoke many associations: hospital wear, uniforms, mummy cloths, bones.

Strips of black tape appear on the faces of the actors during the first section. Here an eye is covered; there a mouth or two eyes. Each taped feature represents the loss of its function.

Nothing more is worn – no jewelry, shoes, or makeup.

The Setting

A proscenium arch or some other well-defined frame reinforces the presentational style of the piece.

Two spotlights, which will later be held by the actors, lie downstage and illuminate the acting area.

Two beds—bare slabs of wood on metal legs—are lined up at the rear.

The beds will be used as pallets for the dying and embalming tables for the dead, as alternate stage levels for the actors to walk upon, as walls, and as graves.

A clothing rack, a large cart, and a ladder are visible.

Stools, equal in number to the actors, stand to the right and left of the stage area in the periphery.

Beneath the stools lie sticks and musical instruments, which will later be used by the actors.

The general effect is deliberately ambiguous. The setting is a theatrical arena, a hospital ward, a graveyard, a nameless home to which people come to die and, perhaps, to be transformed.

44

I. THE CALLING UP OF THE DEAD

Silence.
Overhead lights and two small spots illuminate the beds, the
stools, the empty space.
A trumpet blast.
Music. A light, rhythmic melody.
The actors move to the stools and sit.

SHAMI: We come among the dying to call upon the dead.
There are graves beneath this house—we call upon the dead.
Let them take my body, let them use my tongue.
There are bones beneath this floor—we call upon the dead.
Let the dead come through
                and let it begin with me.

Individual actors begin to join in the calling.
Each carries two sticks, like divining rods.
All the actors eventually participate.
They call up the dead in every corner of the space, facing
each compass point.
Their voices and movements merge and overlap, filling the space
with sounds and words.

THE ACTORS: We come among the dying
   There are bones beneath this floor
     We come among the dying
     We call upon the dead
   There are graves beneath this house
   There are bones beneath this floor
     We call upon the dead
We come
   We come among the dying to call upon the dead
We come
   Let them take my body   We come
Let them take my body, let them use my tongue
   Let the dead come through
Let them take my body, let them use my tongue
   Let the dead come through
Let them take my body, let them use my tongue
     We come among the dying
     There are graves beneath this house
     There are bones beneath this floor

45

Let the dead come through and let it begin with me
     and let it begin with me
     and let it begin with me
Let the dead come through
  Let them take my body
    Let them use my tongue
We come among the dying to call upon the dead
Let the dead come through
  Let the dead come through
    and let it begin with me

The words become increasingly fragmented.
A single syllable evokes the entire incantation.

The sound of the calling becomes its meaning.
Cacophony.

Silence.

Taking In and Eliminating

Two actors stand side by side and squat.

They grimace and contract their pelvic regions.
They simulate defecation.

At the same time, the Patient sits up in bed and chews and swallows.

The Patient swallows regularly, with a gulping sound.

The movements of the ones who are eliminating are in a rhythmic
* relation to the gulping sound of the one who is eating.*

Motion

Three actors come forward.

One runs in place. One turns in a circle.
One runs with the top of his body only.

Breathing

Two actors walk forward, breathing slowly and rhythmically.

One actor gasps in counterpoint to their breath.
Another actor makes a sucking sound; his hands pulsate, feeling
* the air.*

The Last Biological Rites

One actor faces the audience.

A Team Member, impassive and matter-of-fact, stands at his side.

TEAM MEMBER: This is your last chance to use your eyes.

The actor uses his eyes. He looks, he sees. His vision fails. He can see no more.

The Team Member hands him a piece of black tape. The blind man seals off his eyes.

TEAM MEMBER: This is your last chance to use your voice.

The actor makes a sound that presses out into the space and recedes. His voice fades. He can speak no more.

The Team Member hands him a piece of black tape. The dumb man seals off his mouth.

TEAM MEMBER: This is your last chance to use your legs.

The Actor runs in place. He stops.

The Team Member lifts his legs onto a small cart and seats him on his knees.
His chest rises and falls. The only function remaining to him is breathing.

All motion has ceased.

The Team Member and the dying man face the audience.

Tableau.

II. THE STATE OF THE DYING

Darkness.

The actors set up the props for the new section.

Movement and Sound.

The actors return to their stools.

Silence.

Note: *Everyone, except for the dead, is in the state of the dying. For those who are not yet dead, there is always the possibility of change and transformation.*

When the dying allow the dead to inhabit them, they are asking to be moved, to be shifted into a different perspective. To be possessed is to make oneself available to the unknown. At the moments when the dead come through, everything is altered—ideas about life, attitudes toward death, rhythms, sounds, movements. The form of the piece itself must stretch to accommodate these unfamiliar energies.

During this section the two spotlights that have been lying downstage are picked up by the actors and used to illuminate specific aspects of the fragments.

The Dance on the Graves of the Dead

The tableau is interrupted by the voice of one actor who begins the Second Calling.

Others join.

THE ACTORS: We come among the dying
   To call upon the dead.
   There are graves beneath this house.
   There are bones beneath this floor.
      We call upon the dead.
   Let them take my body.
   Let them use my tongue.
   Let the dead come through.
   And let it begin with me.
   We come among the dying
      To call upon the dead.
   There are graves beneath this house.
   There are bones beneath this floor.

48

We call upon the dead
Let the dead come through
Let the dead come through
Let the dead come through
   and let it begin with me
               with me
   Let them take my body
   Let them use my tongue
Let the dead come through and let it begin
   with me   and let it begin with me
     Let them take my body
      and let it begin with me
        Let them use my tongue
         let it begin
Let the dead come through and let it begin
   with me   and let it begin with me   and let it
   Begin

The calling becomes more and more fragmented as the rhythm becomes more and more insistent.

One actor grows silent. Then another. Then all. They collapse from the waist; the sticks dangle from their hands.

Silence.

Drumbeat.

Slowly, one by one, the actors straighten.

They raise their arms still holding the sticks.

The dance begins.

Hands, feet, and sticks drum on every surface. The actors knock on the floor, stools, and beds—on the graves of the dead. They dance individually and in pairs.

From time to time they lie on the floor to let the dead come through.

Dance and knocking merge with fragments from the incantation.

The drumbeat increases in volume.

The dance builds in pace and pitch, reaches a peak, and ceases.

Silence.

Tableau.

The Embalming As Required by Law

The Patient, now inert, is rolled downstage by two Team Members.

Her bed becomes the embalming table.

The Embalmer explains the embalming procedure. A Team Member illustrates the process in gesture and mime.

THE EMBALMER (Tom Lillard): We prepare the deceased for embalming.

The body is washed thoroughly with special attention to the orifices.

A tube is inserted to drain the blood. Through another tube, embalming fluid is injected. As the fluid fills the veins, a flush appears on the face, the eyes flutter, the chest rises and falls giving the appearance of breathing. This is temporary, of course.

An incision is made in the central abdomen. The vital organs are removed and deposited in a bin to be burned. They are replaced by cotton batting, similar to that used in upholstery, to retain the original dimensions of the body. The skin is then repaired and sutured.

Cosmetological procedures are then employed to improve the appearance of the deceased. First is the correction of lip slip.

Lip slip occurs as fluids drain from the upper lip, causing it to recede, forming a sneer. This is unsightly for those viewing the body, so we stitch the lips together into a more attractive expression.

We cut out swollen facial tissue and fill the sunken cheeks by injecting massage creams into them. We then apply conventional makeup, such as rouge and lipstick, to create a natural, lifelike glow.

The body is then dressed in burial garments, which are backless, as the body will be viewed only from above.

The body is now ready to await funeral procedures in the freezer compartment of the morgue.

The Team Members exhibit the newly embalmed body to the Dying by moving it swiftly around the center of the stage.

The Dying sing a ritual farewell song. The melody is light, the pace is lively.

The body is wheeled off.

The Interview

Music is played sporadically throughout the scene.

The actors move to defined areas, each of which represents a different stage in the interviewing process.

TEAM MEMBER A: Hello.

The New Arrival, fully dressed, enters.

NEW ARRIVAL: Hello.

TEAM MEMBER A: Please remove your jacket.

NEW ARRIVAL: Oh, certainly. (*He does so.*)

TEAM MEMBER A: And your shoes, please.

NEW ARRIVAL: My shoes. (*He does so.*)

TEAM MEMBER A: Very good. Nice.

The New Arrival is seated and wheeled to the photographing area.

TEAM MEMBER B: Hello.

NEW ARRIVAL: Hello.

TEAM MEMBER B: We'll take your photograph now.

NEW ARRIVAL: What for?

TEAM MEMBER B: To guide us in restoring your face and body after death.

NEW ARRIVAL: I'd like to look as natural as possible.

TEAM MEMBER B: We know.

Team Member A puts makeup on the New Arrival as Team Member B speaks.

TEAM MEMBER B: That's why we encourage anyone who is dying to spend his last days with us. Everything has been arranged so that, immediately after death, we can move the body from the bed to the embalming table, from the embalming table to the beauty parlor, from the beauty parlor to the coffin.

Team Member A adjusts the New Arrival's position and expression. The photograph is taken.

51

TEAM MEMBER A: Very good. Nice.

The New Arrival is wheeled to the next area.

TEAM MEMBER A: Hello.

NEW ARRIVAL: Hello.

TEAM MEMBER A: Please remove your clothing.

NEW ARRIVAL: My clothing?

TEAM MEMBER A: Those are the instructions. I didn't invent them, they come with the job. Now please remove your clothing.

NEW ARRIVAL: What for?

TEAM MEMBER C: You do want to stay here, don't you?

NEW ARRIVAL: Yes. *(Pause. He undresses.)*

TEAM MEMBER C: Please remove your underwear.

NEW ARRIVAL: I'd like to keep something of my own.

TEAM MEMBER A: We'll give you everything you need. Now please remove your underwear and dress yourself in this garment.

The New Arrival undresses. He is naked for a moment while he puts on the white outfit handed him.

TEAM MEMBER A: Very good. Nice.

The New Arrival is wheeled to the next area.

TEAM MEMBER D: Hello.

NEW ARRIVAL: Hello.

TEAM MEMBER D: Please stand still while your measurements are being taken. Is there anything you need?

NEW ARRIVAL: Yes. I need to be in a bed near a window.

TEAM MEMBER D: You don't need a window. Nobody *needs* a window.

NEW ARRIVAL: I like fresh air. I'd like a window near my bed.

TEAM MEMBER D: We know what you need. That's why we're here.

NEW ARRIVAL: Couldn't you arrange it?

TEAM MEMBER D: Of course, if you really need it.

NEW ARRIVAL: I do.

TEAM MEMBER D: Very good. We do have a bed near a window, but it's in a separate building. The building is a little far away from everything, but we'll be glad to arrange it for you.

NEW ARRIVAL (*after a pause*): There's no one else there?

TEAM MEMBER D: No. None of our other people need a window.

NEW ARRIVAL: Oh. (*Pause.*) Well, then, I guess I could do without it, too.

TEAM MEMBER D: But we'd be glad to arrange it for you if you really need it . . .

NEW ARRIVAL: I wanted to be near a window, but I don't really need it.

TEAM MEMBER D: Very good. You'll be given a bed in the main room with the others.

TEAM MEMBER A: Number 34206.

TEAM MEMBER D: Very nice. Good.

Music.

The Runner Who Never Gets Started
An actor stands sideways on the stage. He runs with the top half of his body only.

The Dead Come Through: Marie Leveau and the Soldier
Let the dead
Let the dead
      dead
Let the dead
      dead

The spirit of Marie Leveau possesses one of the dying.

He breaks into a rhythmic dance and speech.

The entire space becomes charged with the energies of the dead world.

The Soldier marches in place to Marie Leveau's rhythm, then comes through independently.

The dying support and react to the possessed ones with sound and music.

53

MARIE LEVEAU (Paul Zimet):
Eh ye ye Mamzelle Marie
ye ye ye il konin tou
gris gris
li te kouri, aver vieux kokodril
eh oui ye, Mamzelle Marie
Eh ye ye
my people come to me,
they say:

    make that man poor so I grow rich
    make that man die so I can live
    kill my sister
    kill my brother

and no one know the other
and no one see the other

    Marie Leveau, she sees!
    See my people smile,
    and eat each other;
    wipe blood from mouth
    with dainty cloth.

And my ocean stink with dead fish
and my trees are hurt and broken
and my fruit grows sick and rots
and my air is black with poison
that my birds cannot breathe
    and my people eat each other
    and my people live like slaves.

Marie Leveau, she sees!
See my people buying,
see them selling,
see them spending lives
like slaves.
Eh ye ye, Mamzelle Marie
ye ye ye il konin tou
(etc.)

The Soldier moves forward in a march, mouthing "Yessir."
His hand flies to his forehead in repeated salutes.
Marie Leveau grows silent as he speaks.

THE SOLIDER (Jo Ann Schmidman):

Yessir
Yessir
Yessir
Yessir
Yessir

Yes when I wanted to say yes
Yes when I wanted to say no
Yes when I wanted to say yes
Yes when I wanted to say no
Said yes
Said yes
Yessir
Said yes

 And dead because I said yes
 and dead because you said yes
 and dead because I said yes
 and dead because you said yes
And dead before because I never knew why
and dead before because you never asked
And dead before and dead again
dead before and dead again

 Because I never knew

What I was saying yes to!

Said yes
Said yes
Said yes

The Soldier moves to the background but remains visible.
Periodic salutes and "Yessirs" break from him as Marie Leveau comes
through again.

MARIE LEVEAU:

 Marie Leveau, she sees!
 See my people buying, see them selling
 See them spending lives
 like slaves

I see the thief go into business
Now he can steal and not get caught
I see the killer become policeman
Now he can murder, that's his job.

Eh ye ye ye

Marie Leveau, she sees!
See my people smile,
then eat each other;
wipe blood from mouth
with dainty cloth.

And my ocean stink with dead fish
and my trees
and my fruit
and my air
and my birds
and my people eat each other
and my people buy and sell
and my people live
like slaves!

Eh ye ye, Mamzelle Marie
Ye ye ye, il konin tou
(etc.)

The dead depart from the bodies of the possessed.

Sound and movement cease.

Cosmetics

A table, covered with cosmetics and wigs, is rolled onstage.

Two actors begin to beautify themselves; a man and a woman apply makeup and wigs.

The Beautician addresses the audience. She speaks precisely with a minimum of facial or bodily movement.

THE BEAUTICIAN (Jo Ann Schmidman): A beauty parlor and vanity room are connected to the embalming station. We make up the body with conventional cosmetics, restyle the hair, and repair the face.

We clean. We moisturize. We add healthy color to the face. No one is born with perfect features. Are the lips too full? We shape them with lipstick. Are the eyes too small? We add eyeliner, shadow, and false eyelashes. Is the hair skimpy, lifeless? We have wigs in every style and color. Everyone will finally be able to enjoy a perfectly oval, perfectly balanced face.

Generally speaking, we try to avoid a severe or articifial look. Our cosmeticians are trained to produce a natural appearance. Our most attractive models are people who, during their lives, controlled facial expressions and avoided wrinkles by restricting grimaces and smiles to an absolute minimum. Although such people require less attention than those whose faces are marked with laugh lines, creases, and signs of suffering, we can transform anyone. We can erase the lines of a lifetime in less than an hour.

The two actors, completely made up, face the audience.

Spotlights held by two other actors illuminate the transformation.

The Witness

Three actors, different aspects of the Witness, face the audience.

The first actor speaks and repeats the words as the second actor and finally the third interpose their experiences. All three versions rhythmically interweave and overlap.

FIRST ACTOR (Paul Zimet):	SECOND ACTOR (Tina Shepard):	THIRD ACTOR (Shami Chaikin):
Ma, you should get some exercise. Oh, but I do. I go from the kitchen to the bathroom From the bathroom to the bedroom From the bedroom to the living room.	Hi, ma. I see you. (I don't see you dying.)	I saw him lying on his back. Lying there. Like this.
Ma, you should get some exercise.	Hi, ma. I see you. (I don't see you dying.)	Lying there. Like this. Like this.
Oh, but I do. I go from the kitchen to the bathroom From the bathroom to the bedroom From the bedroom to the living room From the kitchen to the bathroom From the bathroom to the bedroom From the bedroom to the living room.	Hi, ma. I see you living. (I don't see you dying.)	Like this.

All the actors become part of the Witness.

They join in the fragments of the speeches, gestures, and movements.

All words and signs become increasingly concentrated and distilled.

The Initiation

The New Arrival stands in the center of a circle of Team Members.

One by one they approach him.

They either slap his face or they embrace him.

There is no apparent reason for their choice.

The New Arrival's breath comes and goes in different rhythms, depending upon whether he has been slapped or embraced.

The Dead Come Through: The Responsible One
The spirit of The Responsible One possesses one of the dying.

THE RESPONSIBLE ONE (Tina Shepard): I was walking down the street
Cracks in the sidewalk.
I saw a man.
Cracks in his face.
    What have I done?

I saw a child choking on air.
    What have I done?
Oceans rising.
    What have I done?
Buildings toppled.
    What have I done?

What was given me was impossible to work with.

I saw a woman
no teeth
nibbling at the pavement
chewing at the pavement
mouth full of stone.
    What have I done?

I saw snow falling.
flakes of sky.
    What have I done?
Forty-one dead.

What have I done?

I saw.
I saw.
I can't say I didn't.
What have I done?

Sitting.
Standing.
Sleeping.
Sleepwalking.

What was given me was impossible to work with.

Blood.
    What have I done?
Fire. A man on fire.
    What have I done?
I saw—agh!
    What have I done?
I saw—kkk!
    What have I done?
Ahhhhhhh!
    What have I done?
Bkhhhhhh!
    What have I done?

What was given me was impossible to work with.

The Interview

The New Arrival is led to another area.

Two Team Members await him. One stands on a ladder, holding a stick. Another questions him.

Each time he gives an incorrect answer, the sound of the stick cutting through air is heard. As he hits the New Arrival, the Team Member utters a cry of pain.

TEAM MEMBER: Did you like it?

NEW ARRIVAL: Like it? (*He is hit.*)

TEAM MEMBER: Did you like it?

NEW ARRIVAL: No. (*He is hit.*)

TEAM MEMBER: Did you like it?

NEW ARRIVAL: I'll say I liked it if you want me to. (*He is hit.*)

TEAM MEMBER: Did you like it?

NEW ARRIVAL: Yes. I liked it.

TEAM MEMBER: Do you mean it?

NEW ARRIVAL: What's the difference? (*He is hit.*)

TEAM MEMBER: Do you mean it?

NEW ARRIVAL: Yes. I mean it.

TEAM MEMBER: So you liked it.

NEW ARRIVAL: Yes. I liked it.

TEAM MEMBER: And you mean it.

NEW ARRIVAL: Yes. I mean it.

TEAM MEMBER: Why did you like it?

NEW ARRIVAL: I don't know. (*He is hit.*)

TEAM MEMBER: Why did you like it?

NEW ARRIVAL: I liked it because it was different. (*He is hit.*)

TEAM MEMBER: Why did you like it?

NEW ARRIVAL: I liked it because I never . . . (*He is hit.*)

TEAM MEMBER: Why did you like it?

NEW ARRIVAL: I liked it because it was necessary to like it.

The Dying Pray

The actors improvise a dance. They jam vocally and with handheld instruments. They are completely caught up in the sound and movement They are acting out their prayer.

The Dead Come Through: The Executed Man and the Song

A bed is raised and stood upright. A woman stands flattened against it, gripping its sides.

She rocks from left to right; the bed knocks against the floor on each side.

The Executed Man comes through.

THE EXECUTED MAN (Raymond Barry):

My eyes. Wide open.
My head. Full of imagination.
Like when I was a kid.
Free in the head.

Like me and my friend, Joel, we used to fish in a place called "the pit." The water there was so clear you could see the fish swimming—big, beautiful fish. We used to cut off their heads and rip out their stomachs and tear the scales off them. Yeah, me and Joel, we had fantastic imaginations.

I was sentenced—
just like you!

Warden!
I know you got that noose ready for me
but it's that noose that's set me free
A man who knows he's gonna die
doesn't have anything to be afraid of.

My prison's made of steel;
yours is in your head.

If someone came into our pit me and Joel knew how to fix him. We'd take a wire and wrap it 'round his cock and we'd twist it and twist it and twist it till that fella hollered—MAAAAAAAAA!

I was sentenced—
just like you!

But that warden he gets up real early in the morning and he looks at himself in the mirror and says, What a good man I am! Me, I knew I'd end up with my head in a noose. That's why I could say:

Yes!
I am a thief.
Yes!
I am an addict.
Yes!
I am a pimp, a rapist.
Yes!
I am a murderer.

Everything I imagine is part of me.

I was sentenced—
just like you!

Go on, warden, be good, be nice, do what you're told. You've been
sentenced just like me, but you've kept that locked up, too.

My prison's made of steel;
yours is in your head!

*The sound of the wooden bed rocking against the floor grows louder.
The song fills the woman; it uses her voice to sing itself.*

*The words of the song are repeated over and over again with various
intentions.*

*The meaning of the words is secondary to the range of human emotions
that can be expressed through them.*

THE SONG (Shami Chaikin): A-nee Ma-a-meen
A-nee Ma-a-meen
A-nee Ma-a-meen

A-nee Ma-a-meen
A-nee Ma-a-meen
A-nee Ma-a-meen
  (*etc.*)
The song and the rocking end abruptly.

The Embalming as Required by Law

A living person is placed on the embalming table.

The Embalmers perform their jobs as before.

*The victim screams and writhes. His energies gradually dissipate; when
his mouth is sewn, he grows completely silent.*

62

THE EMBALMER (Tom Lillard): We prepare the deceased for embalming.

The body is washed thoroughly with special attention to the orifices.

A tube is inserted to drain the blood. Through another tube, embalming fluid is injected. As the fluid fills the veins, a flush appears on the face, the eyes flutter, the chest rises and falls giving the appearance of breathing. This is temporary, of course.

An incision is made in the central abdomen. The vital organs are removed and deposited in a bin to be burned. They are replaced by cotton batting, similar to that used in upholstery, to retain the original dimensions of the body. The skin is then repaired and sutured.

Cosmetological procedures are then employed to improve the appearance of the deceased. First is the correction of lip slip.

Lip slip occurs when fluids drain from the upper lip, causing it to recede, forming a sneer. This is unsightly for those viewing the body, so we stitch the lips together into a more attractive expression.

We cut out swollen facial tissues, fill the sunken cheeks by injecting massage creams into them. We then apply conventional makeup, such as rouge and lipstick, to create a natural and lifelike glow.

The body is then dressed in burial garments, which are backless, as the body will be viewed from above only.

The body is now ready to await funeral procedures in the freezer compartment of the morgue.

The person on the embalming table is now silent and motionless.

The body is wheeled off. The farewell melody is played.

The Dying Imagine Their Judgment

Center-stage, a ladder with a horn and megaphone.

An empty chair at the side.

A rack toward the rear.

The Judge (Shami Chaikin) *climbs the ladder and sits on the highest rung. She holds a book, from which she reads the judgments.*

The Judge speaks in the impersonal voice of a radio broadcaster; in a hoarse, authoritarian rasp; in a tired whine.

The judgments are pronounced in a continuous, repetitive loop; a variety of images are enacted at the same time.

The judge blows the horn and begins.

The Judgments

The judgment of your life is your life.

You will finally possess the thing you wanted most in life—and eternity will be that thing and that thing only.

You are in the death of crowds. There are multitudes about you and they are, each one, yourself. There is not one other besides you—and yet, there are multitudes.

There is a space between what was done and what could have been done and you are rooted in that space. The judgment of your life is your life.

You are standing in a space filled with bodies and you watch their couplings and breathe their odors, but you cannot touch them and they will not reach out to you.

You saw, you saw, you can't say you didn't. The judgment of your life is your life.

You moved from the house to the office, from the office to the house; from sleep to waking and from waking to sleep; you moved from yesterday to today, from today to tomorrow—and you will repeat that movement for eternity.

Did you sit on another's head or were you sat upon? Either way, you will never be free of the one who is above or the one who is below. The judgment of your life is your life.

The Images

The musician sits at a typewriter and for the duration of the scene makes a record of the proceedings.

An actor pushes two bodies on the embalming table around the space.

An actor sits on a cart, her head between the metal bars.

An actor kneels on a small cart and wheels herself with her hands.

An actor seated on a large cart is pushed by another actor.

They are followed by another actor with tape over his eyes who is kneeling on the small cart and pushing himself with his hands.

Two actors hang upside down from a rack and breathe heavily. They are pushed across the stage.

An actor follows on the small cart. There is tape over his mouth.

An actor running in place on the large cart is wheeled around the space.

You are standing on a bridge, but
you do not know it. All around
you, people come onto it and
pass off of it, but you do not
understand that all those who
walk upon it at the same time
are not strangers.

You neither faced your death
nor participated in your life,
but straddled the line between
one place and the other, longing
for both. The judgment of your
life is your life.

You will finally possess the thing
you wanted most in life— and
eternity will be that thing and
that thing only.

You are in the death of crowds.
There are multitudes about you
and they are, each one, youself.
There is not one other besides
you—and yet there are multitudes.

There is a space between what
was done and what could have
been done and you are rooted in
that space. The judgment of your
life is your life.

You are standing in a space filled
with bodies and you watch their
couplings and breathe their odors,
but you cannot touch them and
they will not reach out to you.

You saw, you saw, you can't say
you didn't. The judgment of your
life is your life.

You moved from the house to
the office, from the office to the
house, from sleep to waking and
from waking to . . . .
. . . .

*Another actor hangs upside down
on the rack and is pushed by two
others.*

*An actor climbs the ladder and
whispers in the judge's ear. He
looks around at the audience
and whispers in her ear again.*

*A chain of people crawl beneath
the ladder on their bellies. They
propel themselves forward by
movements of their hips, arms,
and legs. They seem to be swimming.*

*A continuous bubble of sound
dribbles from their lips as they
crawl.*

*When the first person has moved
as far forward as possible, he/she
branches to the right or left.
Still on his/her belly, he/she
struggles to the end of the line
and repeats the seemingly endless
passage.*

The Judge grows tired.

*The stream of human souls contin-
ues to pass beneath the ladder.*

*The voice of the Judge slurs
and fades.*

She is almost asleep.

The chain continues beneath her.

[black out]

Terminal Portfolio by Max Waldman

The Calling Up of the Dead (Raymond Barry, Paul Zimet, Jo Ann Schmidman)

Marie Laveau (Paul Zimet

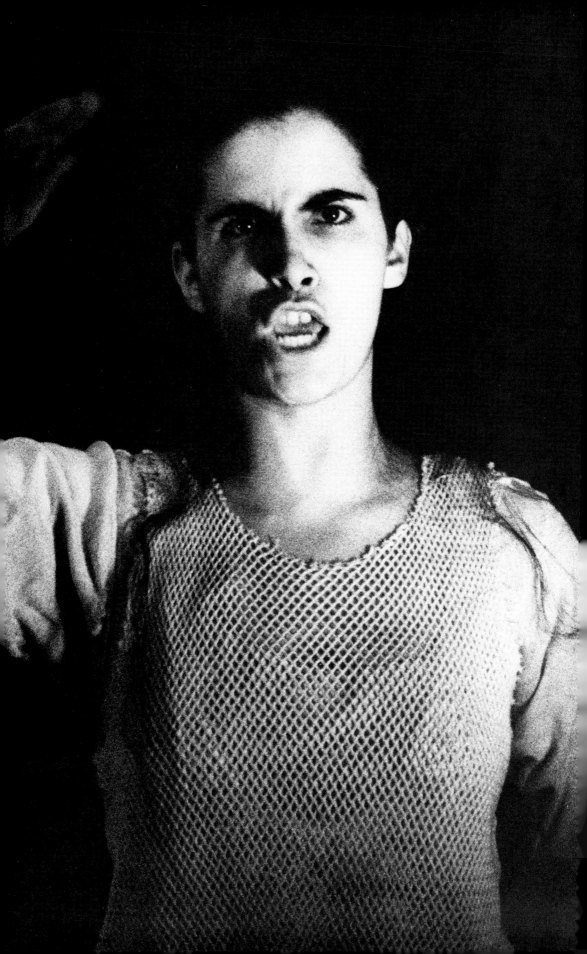

Soldier (Jo Ann Schmidman)

The Dance on the Graves of the Dead (Tina Shepard, Tom Lillard,
Raymond Barry, Paul Zimet, Shami Chaikin, Jo Ann Schmidman)

79

The Dead Come Through (Shami Chaikin, Raymond Barry, Paul Zimet)

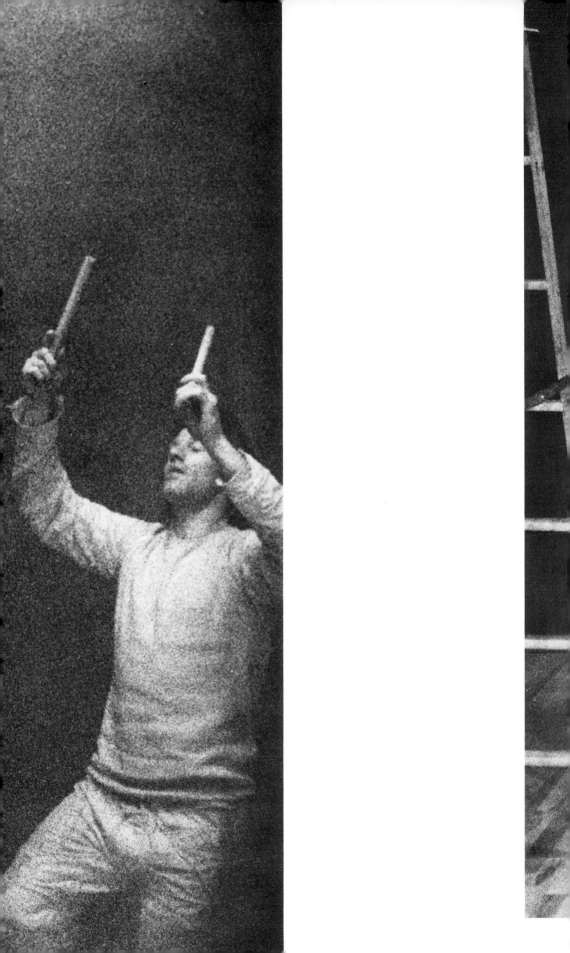

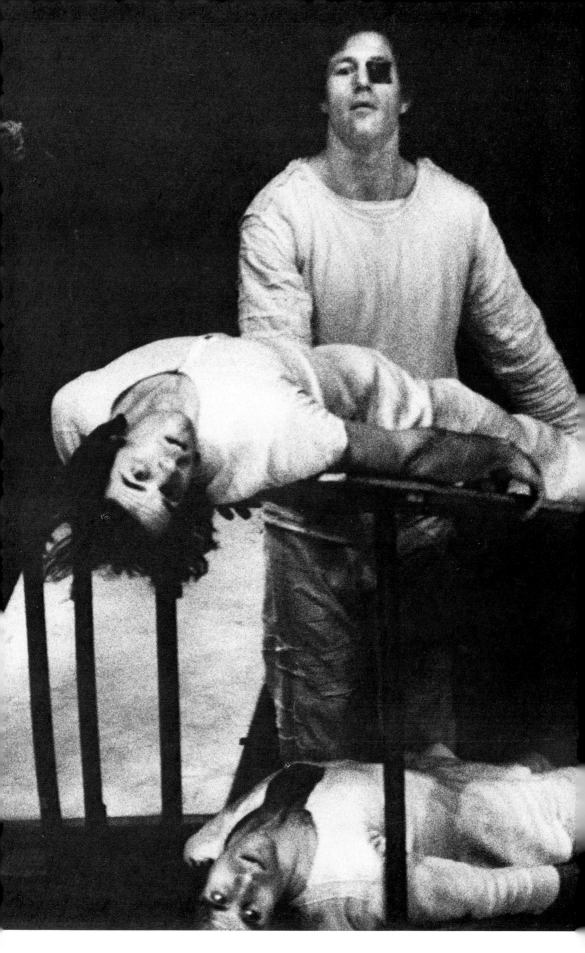

The Judgments (Shami Chaikin, Tina Shepard, Jo Ann Schmidman)

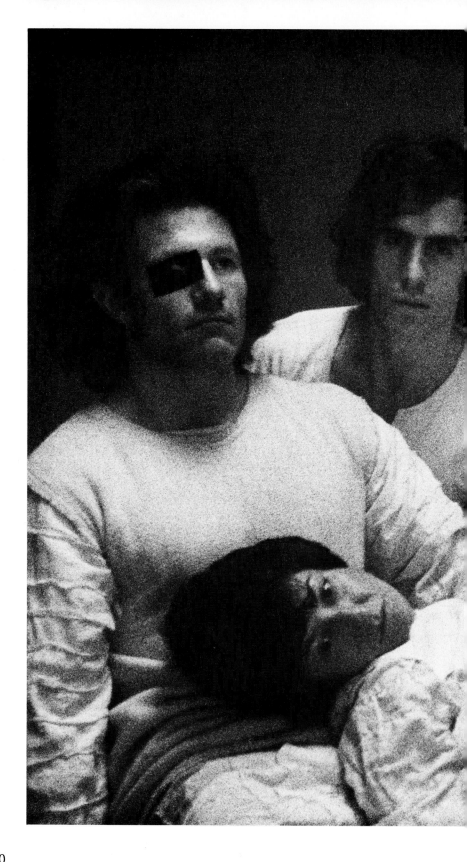

Shami Chaikin, Raymond Barry, Paul Zimet, Tom Lillard, Tina Shepard, Jo Ann Schmidman

The Mutation Show

THE MUTATION SHOW

co-directed by
JOSEPH CHAIKIN and ROBERTA SKLAR

The Ensemble:
   Raymond Barry
   Shami Chaikin
   Tom Lillard
   Jo Ann Schmidman
   Tina Shepard
   Paul Zimet

Musician:
   Ellen Maddow

Administrative director:
   John Stoltenberg

Production managers:
   Michael Bartuccio and Stephen Rich

Administrative assistant:
   Patricia Berman

Costumes:
   Gwen Fabricant

Lighting designed by:

   Arden Fingerhut

Setting designed by:
   Bil Mikulewicz

Music consultant:
   Stanley Walden

Writer-in-residence
October 1970 to June 1971:
   W.E.R. LaFarge

Writer-in-residence September 1971 to March 1972:
   John Stoltenberg

THE SEQUENCE

*(Only those segments containing words
have been included in The Sequence.)*

I
RULES FOR THE AUDIENCE

ELLEN:
We'd like to ask you to observe the following rules.
No smoking.
No taking pictures.
No crinkling paper.
No firearms.
Make arrangements for sharing your
   armrests (or legroom).
Try to avoid having sexual fantasies
   about the people in the play.
Try to avoid having sexual fantasies
   about the person to the right
   or left of you.
Try to think up a comment during the play
   so you can have an opinion
   later.

II
THE MUTANT GALLERY

SHAMI:
The Bird Lady: She wiggles and she writhes and she writhes and she
    wiggles. The bird lady.
The Man Who Smiles: He moves and moves and smiles and smiles. He's
    never stopped moving. The man who smiles.
The Man Who Hits Himself: He's had the same nightmare for 35 years.
    The man who hits himself.
The Thinker: She thinks she thinks, but she doesn't know what it is
    that she thinks. The thinker.
The Petrified Man.
The Bird Lady: She was conceived one winter night when a farm boy
    raped an ostrich. The bird lady.
The Man Who Smiles: He's never stopped moving, he's never stopped
    smiling. If he didn't smile, he'd have no face. The man who
    smiles.
The Man Who Hits Himself: He's had the same nightmare for 35 years.
    The man who hits himself.
The Thinker: She thinks she thinks, but she doesn't know what it is
    that she thinks. The thinker.
The Petrified Man: He's always under attack. Each day he moves less
    and talks less. The petrified man.

The Bird Lady: She's half woman and half bird.
The Man Who Smiles; He's never stopped.
The Man Who Hits Himself: He hits himself and hits himself.
The Thinker: She thinks up thoughts. There goes one now.
The Petrified Man: Each day he moves less.

The Bird Lady.
The Man Who Smiles.
The Man Who Hits Himself.
The Thinker.
The Petrified Man.

III
THE BOY IN THE BOX

SHAMI:
The Boy in the Box.
He lived alone in his box all his days.
He never saw distance, light, the night sky, or another person.
One day he was torn from his box and carried to a hill where he was left.

IV
THE ANIMAL GIRL

SHAMI:
The Animal Girl.
She was raised with animals.
She ate and drank and slept with an animal pack.
One day she was torn from her cave, and carried away, and made
    civilized.

V
ROPES
(chant)

SHAMI:
We will name her.
We will straighten her bones.
We will give her words.
We will caress her.
We will name her.
We will straighten her bones.
We will give her words.
We will caress her.
We will dress her.
We will train her.
We will name her.
We will name her.
We will name her.

97

VI
BREAKING OUT OF THE BOX AND SEEING

RAY:

Nothing with me in my box all the time closed I was still alone with only my fluids came out of here and here and here and here and here and then out of the box I saw for the first time only that one time saw light light light coming into my head from long time away moving and turning seeing long poles with green at the top hitting against my face and I saw another box the top was blue the bottom was many colors it had many colors moving and turning and then I saw and then I saw you and I saw you and I saw you seeing and then trying to stand falling saw stars moving across the light in front of the long time and many boxes with holes and people going in and out of the holes and when they moved it made a noise and the noise was in my head and the noise was me and I saw the boxes and I saw the noise. I don't know if this happened to me or to someone else but I know it happened.

VII
WALKING IN SHOES
(chant refrain)

SHAMI:
We will name her.
We will caress her.
We will name her.
We will caress her.
We will name her.
We will name her.
We will name her.

VIII
WEDDING DANCE

ELLEN:

The bride is now dancing with the groom.

The groom is now dancing with the mother of the bride.

The bride is now dancing with the father of the groom.

The bride is now dancing with the mother of the groom.

The groom is now dancing with the father of the bride.

The groom is now dancing with the daughter of the bride.

The daughter of the bride is now dancing with the grandfather of the groom.

The third cousin of the bride is now dancing with the great uncle of the groom.

The mother of the bride is now dancing with the mayor.

The father of the groom is now dancing with the captain of police.

The bride is now dancing with the secretary of affairs.

The minister of information is now dancing with the sister of the bride.

The President is now dancing with his assassin.

The cow is now dancing with the butcher.

The butcher is now dancing with the people.

The judges are now dancing with each other.

The king is now dancing with the oil men.

The oil men are now dancing with the generals.

The people are now dancing with the laws.

The dead are now dancing with the newborn.

The trees are now dancing with the wind.

The earth is now dancing with the stars.

IX
THE HUMAN GALLERY

ELLEN:
I am Ellen Maddow. I am 5′5″ tall. I have dark hair and dark eyes.
Jo Ann Schmidman is 5′6″ tall and has long, dark hair.
Shami Chaikin has dark hair, a dark complexion, and is 5′4″ tall.
Paul Zimet is tall, thin, and has dark hair.
Tom Lillard has a barrel chest, slim hips, and sandy-colored hair.
Tina Shepard is short, has short blonde hair and blue eyes.
Ray Barry is 6′2″, weighs 187 pounds and has blue eyes.
Jo Ann Schmidman was born in Omaha, Nebraska. She is 25 years old.
Tom Lillard was born in Duck River, Tennessee. When he was 18 he
joined the marines.
Tina Shepard is the daughter of Jean (deceased) and Bill; stepdaughter
of Jane; stepdaughter of Gil (deceased); sister of Joan (married); half-
sister of Connie, Sally, Billy, Betsy, Susan, and David; niece of Fran
and Alan (divorced), Marny and Bob, and Betty and John; aunt of Marc
and Duncan; cousin of Chris, Bruce, Emily, Alice, Trina, Sarah, Robby,
Carly, Susan, Dick, and John; second cousin of David and Elaine; third
cousin of Leonard and Paula.
Ray Barry was employed as a gardener, a cook, a waiter, a busboy, a
dishwasher, a longshoreman, a construction worker, an English teacher,
a social worker, and a sculptor.
Tina Shepard's uncle John is a federal judge.
Tom Lillard's cousin Fred is a Ku Klux Klansman.
In the sixth grade Paul Zimet won the American Legion Citizenship
Award.

X
THE MUTANTS GIVE TESTIMONY

TINA:
I swear to tell the whole truth and nothing but.
This is not my voice.
What's happening.
What's happening.
To tell.
I swear to tell.
The whole truth.
I swear.
This is not my voice.

PAUL:
I speak it the way I hear it.
I see it the way it was shown to me.
I do it the way I was taught it.
Why did they teach me to speak this way
    if I was not meant to be a clergyman?
What do you see when you look at me?
What do you think I see when I look at you?

The Mutation Show Portfolio
by Mary Ellen Mark

Tom Lillard, Jo Ann Schmidman, Raymond Barry, Tina Shepard, Paul Zimet, Ellen Maddow, Shami Ch

106

The Journey (Paul Zimet, Raymond Barry

The Animal Pack (Tom Lillard, Shami Chaikin, Paul Zimet,
Jo Ann Schmidman, Raymond Barry, Tina Shepard)

Breaking Out of the Box and Seeing (Raymond Barry)

116

Raymond Barry, Paul Zimet, Tina Shepard, Tom Lillard

Couples (Shami Chaikin, Tom Lillard)

Tina Shepard, Paul Zimet

Jo Ann Schmidman, Tom Lillard

123

Shami Chaikin

Raymond Barry, Tina Shepard, Shami Chaikin

The Wedding Danc

The Human Gallery (Raymond Barry, Tina Shepard, Tom Lillard, Paul Zimet, Shami Chaikin, Jo Ann Schmidman, Ellen Maddow)

The Mutants Give Testimony (Tom Lillard,
Shami Chaikin, Tina Shepard)

Nightwalk

NIGHTWALK

directed by
JOSEPH CHAIKIN

Contributing writers:
  Jean-Claude van Itallie
  Sam Shepard
  Megan Terry

The Ensemble:
  Raymond Barry
  Shami Chaikin
  Ralph Lee
  Tom Lillard
  Ellen Maddow
  Jo Ann Schmidman
  Tina Shepard
  Paul Zimet

Administrative director:
  John Stoltenberg

Production manager:
  Michael Bartuccio

Administrative assistant:
  Patricia Berman

Production director:
  Stephen Rich

Dramaturge:
  Mira Rafalowicz

Costumes:
  Gwen Fabricant

Lighting designed by:
  Arden Fingerhut

Setting designed by:
  Michael Bartuccio

Sound consultant:
  Susan Ain

Writer-in-residence:
  Jean-Claude van Itallie

Lines from "On the Road Home" by Wallace Stevens.
Lines from "Crow's Account of the Battle" by Ted Hughes.
Song, "Long Time Gone," by Bob Dylan.

THE SEQUENCE

(Some of the segments indicated in The Sequence have no words.)

I. THE JOURNEY BEGINS
    A. The Traveler Prepares
    B. The Creature Explores

II. IMAGES
    A. Men's World
    B. Tom's Roar
    C. The Couple's World

III. THE PEOPLE'S INDICTMENT
    by Jean-Claude van Itallie

IV. NOW I AM

V. THE TRAVELER AND THE CREATURE DANCE

VI. IMAGES
    A. Men's World
    B. Women's World

VII. THE HOUSE AND THE FISH
    by Sam Shepard

VIII. CONVERSATION

IX. DINNER WITH THE BOSS
    by Megan Terry

X. NOW I AM

XI. THE SLEEP WORLD

XII. THE TRAVELER AND THE CREATURE ARE LOST AND FOUND
    A. The Chase
    B. The Dance
    C. The Traveler's Chant

XIII. THE SONG WORLD
    A. "A Long Time Gone" by Bob Dylan
    B. "My Defenses Are Down" by Irving Berlin
    C. "I'm In the Mood for Love" by Jimmy McHugh and Dorothy Fields
    D. "Violate Me in the Violet Time" by Allie Wrubel and Robert Wrubel
    E. "Every Time We Say Goodbye" by Cole Porter
    F. "Embraceable You" by Cole Porter

XIV. THE SONGSTRESS AND THE TRAMP

XV. THE CLOWNS' WORLD
    A. Now I Am
    B. Talking Carts

XVI. THE CREATURE TRIES ON THE CHARACTERS

XVII. THE BATTLE OF CREATURES

XVIII. THE TRAVELER'S SPEECH

XIX. PICTURE OF PEOPLE

XX. THE TAMBOURINE PLAYER

XXI. RAY'S SPEECH

XXII. THE TRAVELER AND THE CREATURE WALK

III. THE PEOPLE'S INDICTMENT

TOM: Indictment

SHAMI: Indictment to God.

ELLEN: Just say "Indictment." No "to God."

TOM (reading): It is *You* —

SHAMI: Did you capitalize that?

TOM: Capitalized it. Yes. Why?

JO ANN: Don't capitalize "*you*."

TOM: Yes, well . . . (He continues to read)
      You, lower case, are accused.

RALPH: Not "*you*." "*him*."

SHAMI: "*Him*?"

RALPH: Speak to *him* in the third person. *He* is "The Accused."

JO ANN: Only speak of *him*, not to *him*.

ELLEN: Speak to *him*, not of *him*. It is to *him* that we are speaking.
      We are not conversing among ourselves. We are drafting
      an indictment.

JO ANN: If we speak to *him* rather than of *him* we recognize *him*.

ELLEN: But we can't say anything to him without saying anything to
      him!

JO ANN: Well, then let it be the last time we speak.

SHAMI: Unless *he* answers.

ELLEN: *He* hasn't ever answered before.

TOM: The Accused is not present.

RALPH: Nonetheless we accuse *him*. Let us keep our minds, friends, to
      the matter. "We accuse you, sir!" Write that down.

TOM: "We accuse you, sir!"

ELLEN: It is *you* —

SHAMI: It is *you*, who is not present —

TOM: It is *you* who is not present who gives me the appetite to eat the
      flesh of my fellows.

SHAMI: It is *you* who gives me consciousness and who drugs my mind
      into sleep at once.

ELLEN: Not "at once." Say "simultaneously."

TOM: Simultaneously *you* give me consciousness and *you* drug me.

ELLEN: I don't like "consciousness."

TOM: *You* waken me and you put me to sleep.

ELLEN: Simultaneously.

SHAMI: *You* —

ELLEN: Who?

TOM: *You*, who we are calling The Accused, it is your spell which conjures in me an apparition of *you*.

JO ANN: You cause me to dream *you*.

TOM: *you* —

ELLEN: *he* —

TOM: Is the absence I have lived with always.

RALPH: *You* are the absence I have lived with always.

JO ANN: It is *you*.

ELLEN: *him*.

JO ANN: It is not *"him."* *He* is not. We accuse *you* of having never been been.

TOM: *You* mock us.

RALPH: *You* create forms and the illusions of forms.

TOM: *His* crimes call for a punishment corresponding.

JO ANN: There is no such punishment.

SHAMI: We must put *you* to sleep as you have done unto us.

JO ANN: We must forget *him* as *he* has forgotten us.

RALPH: We accuse *you*. And we try *you* despite *your* silence. And we will answer *your* silence with our own.

JO ANN: Henceforth shall *he* be Nameless.

TOM: I forget *you*. *You* who have never lived will no longer be a dream in the minds of the living.

SHAMI: This indictment —

ELLEN: Accusation —

JO ANN: Document —

RALPH: We now tear up before your unseeing eyes.

ELLEN: Unseen.

TOM: And we forget *you*.

SHAMI: *He* is forgotten. . .

TOM: And we shall make no reference to *you*.

RALPH: There is no one to be remembered.

JO ANN: No indictment was delivered.

SHAMI: We recognize nothing to deliver it to.

TOM: We deliver this indictment to nothing. And we forget *him*.

RALPH: It is forgotten.

IV. NOW I AM

RAY: Now I am in the process of talking

SHAMI: Now I am sitting

RAY: Now I am in the process of walking

SHAMI: Now I am standing

RAY: Now I am in the process of eating

SHAMI: Now I am turning and saying these words

RAY: Now I am in the process of sleeping

SHAMI: Now I am sitting down

RAY: Now I am in the process of being flamboyant

SHAMI: Now I am standing up

RAY: Now I am in the process of fighting

SHAMI: Now I am sitting down

RAY: Now I am in the process of talking

VII. THE HOUSE AND THE FISH

RAY: In my house the night moves in.
The air's changed.
The water moves in the pipes.
Somebody's taking a bath.
I see myself on a ship at night staring out to the lights on the shore.
One of the lights is me.
Me in my house.
Me on the ship at night staring out to myself in the house.

Below the sea is a blind fish.
A long snake fish with blank gray eyes.
Me in the ship is imagining him down there.
He goes on sucking the bottom.
I'm inside that fish.
I sink, I sink.
I don't want to die in my sleep.

The ship cuts me off from the house.
The house from the fish.
I'm inside that fish.

IX. DINNER WITH THE BOSS

(Most of this scene is played with nonsense syllables in place of words. The actors' "mode" makes the intention clear.)

Seating

JO ANN (HOSTESS): Now — you sit there on the Boss's right. He likes a pretty face with his meal.

TOM (BOSS): Haw, haw, haw.

HOSTESS: And we can't have all the girls together, can we? Now we have boy, girl, boy, girl, boy, girl.

BOSS: I think you've started something. Haw, haw, haw.

Admiring the Table

ELLEN (GUEST 1): Crocus . . . I didn't know they were up yet. . .

Praying

Carving

HOSTESS: We're ready for you to carve, dear.

BOSS: So am I.

ELLEN AND RALPH (GUESTS 1 AND 2): Biggest we ever saw.

Passing

GUEST 2: Shall I start passing the . . .

HOSTESS: Of course.

GUESTS: Pass, pass, pass, pass . . .

BOSS: Name yer poison. White? Dark? Who gets rare?

RAY (GUEST 3): I do.

BOSS: Who likes crispy fat?

GUESTS 1 AND 2: We like crispy fat.

BOSS: Can you rassle a bone?

Compliments to the Hostess

HOSTESS: Dive in. Eat while it's hot. I didn't slave over a hot stove just so's you could look at it.

GUEST 2: Do you care which fork?

HOSTESS: God invented fingers first.

Man Talk

BOSS: Hey, Ralph, did you call that S.O.B. in Cleveland?

GUEST 2: Like clockwork.

BOSS: Snow him.

GUEST 2: I snowed him so good he doubled his last year's orders.

BOSS: Perfect, now we got liquid cash flow to expand.

GUEST 3: Hot damn, I can tool up the new plant

143

BOSS: Yer damn tootin'.

GUEST 3: Makes my mouth water.

BOSS: We are gonna go with this boom boys. I can feel it in my bones. There's no end in sight.

GUEST 3: The boom's been building.

BOSS: Them idiots been peddling gloom are gonna be out in the cold.

GUEST 2: And we eat good.

BOSS: You damn right we eat good. We eat good like this all the time. That plant at the Mexican border. It took five men to do the work of one white man.

Man's Story *(Boasting mode)*

Insults

GUESTS 1 AND 2: Longhaired, filthy, child-molesting faggots wearing come-smeared leather sex clothes, moved into our neighborhood, jerk each other's diseased bodies off in the commie pinko parked cars and corrupt our sweet-breathed children into their corrupt cocksucking, ass-rimming, motherfucking, degenerate rituals. Sex dance every night in the sexed-up streets. Fucking and sucking and ramming and jamming degenerate sex parts and living farts in every part and place of the dogshit streets. Motherfucking cocksuckers dishing in doorways. Faggots free-fucking in eyes and ears!

HOSTESS: Some green for your plates. A pretty plate means well balanced.

Tantrum

RAY TO SHAMI: *mode — most important dinner . . .*
mode — wait till we get home. . . .

HOSTESS: *mode — boss likes meat for his meal . . .*
Excuse me for a minute please.

Dessert

HOSTESS: Surprise. Surprise. Sweet tooth. Surprise for everyone with a clean plate.

GUEST 3: Pumpkinpie. Pumpkinpie.

HOSTESS: Do you want it? Do you want it? Do you want it? A slice for you and a slice for you and a slice for you and a slice for me and a slice for the boss.

GUESTS 1 AND 2: Melts in our mouth.

Compliments

GUEST 1: You must have worked all day yesterday and all day today to make this beautiful food.

144

X. NOW I AM

RAY: Now I am sleeping
SHAMI: Now I am sitting
RAY: Now I am in sleep
SHAMI: Now I am standing
RAY: Now I am talking in the voices of sleepers
SHAMI: Now I am turning and saying these words
RAY: Now I am sleeping
SHAMI: Now I am sitting down
RAY: Now I am in sleep

XII(C). THE TRAVELER'S CHANT

(A Navajo Indian Chant)

PAUL:
In beauty I walk
with beauty before me I walk
with beauty behind me I walk
with beauty above me I walk
with beauty above and about me I walk
in beauty I walk
with beauty before me I walk
with beauty behind me I walk
with beauty above me I walk
with beauty above and about me I walk
in beauty I walk
with beauty before me I walk
with beauty behind me I walk
with beauty above and about me I walk

XIII. THE SONG WORLD

A. A Long Time Gone

SHAMI:

My parents raised me tenderly
I was their only one
My mind got mixed with rambling
When I was so young
I left my home for the first time
When I was twelve and one
I'm a long time in coming
And I'll be a long time gone.

Many times by the highway
I tried to flag a ride
With bloodshot eyes and gritting teeth
I watched the cars roll by
I banged my head against the wind
And shouted at a stone
I'm a long time in coming
And I'll be a long time gone.

You might see me at your crossroads
When I am passing through
Remember me how you wish to
As I'm drifting from your view
I haven't got time to think about it
I've got too much to get done
I'm a long time in coming
And I'll be a long time gone.
I'm a long time in coming
And I'll be a long time gone.
I'm a long time in coming
And I'll be a long time gone.

B. My Defenses Are Down

C. I'm in the Mood for Love

D. Violate Me in the Violet Time

E. Every Time We Say Goodbye

F. Embraceable You

146

XIV. THE SONGSTRESS AND THE TRAMP
In the Garden

JO ANN:
I come to the garden alone
While the dew is still on the roses,
And the voice I hear falling on my ear
The Son of God discloses.

And he walks with me and he talks with me,
He tells me I am his own;
And the joys we share
As we tarry there
None other has ever known.

He speaks, and the sound of his voice
Is so sweet that the birds hush their singing,
And the melody that he gives to me
Within my heart is ringing.

And he walks with me and he talks with me,
He tells me I am his own;
And the joys we share
As we tarry there
None other has ever known.

I stay in the garden with him,
Though the night about me be falling,
And he bids me go though the voice of woe
His voice to me is calling.

And he walks with me and he talks with me,
He tells me I am his own;
And the joys we share . . .

147

XV. THE CLOWNS' WORLD

(The action is simultaneous
The actors' lines alternate.)

RAY:
Now I am being flamboyant
Now I am blowing my whistle
Now I am showing you my behind
Now I am being flamboyant . . .

ELLEN:
Now I am washing the dishes
Now I am making the bed
Now I am brushing my teeth
Now I am thinking big thoughts
Now I am walking

SHAMI and RALPH (in one pair of pants):
Now I am walking forwards
Now I am walking backwards
Now I am scratching my ass
Now I am putting on my hat
Now I am taking off my hat
Now I am walking off

RAY: Now I am leaving flamboyantly

ELLEN: Now I am walking off

XVIII. THE TRAVELER'S SPEECH

PAUL:

Hold on to my hand
And all the night the light was changing
And there's himself and herself
One dies and the next one watches
Then that one dies and the next one watches him
Then that one dies and another watches him
We've taken a lot of pictures
At the edge of the world
There's himself and yourself
Hold on to my hand
And all the night the light was changing
Now I'm holding your hand
Now I'm walking
At the edge of the world
Now I'm sleeping and saying these words
There's yourself and herself and this creature
You are the other part of me
At the edge of the world
"It was when I said there is no such thing as truth
that the grapes seemed fatter, the fox ran out of his hole."[1]
Hold on to my hand.
"It was at that time that the silence was largest and longest."[1]
We want to have a swim. We want to take a walk.
We're having a wonderful time.
There's yourself and myself and this apple and a blind fish.
I'll show you people and pieces of people
A piece for you and a piece for me
"It was at that time that the silence was largest and longest
It was at that time that the night was roundest."[1]
Hold on to my hand
"At the edge of the world"[2]
"There was this terrific battle
The noise was as much as the possible limits of noise could take
It outlasted many prayers
Till the explosives ran out
And what was left looked around at what was left."[3]
We're having a wonderful time
We've taken a lot of pictures.
"At the edge of the world it looks calm."[2]
We want to swim. We want to walk. We want to ride a bike.
"At the edge of the world it breathes like a monster
At the edge of the world it holds me.
At the edge of the world I'm waiting to fall.
At the edge of the world it lets me tremble."[2]
Hold on to my hand
"At the edge of the world it holds me trembling."[2]

[1]Wallace Stevens, "On the Road Home"   [2]Sam Shepard
[3]Ted Hughes, "Crow's Account of the Battle"

XXI. RAY'S SPEECH

There was himself and herself and herself and himself

and between us

there was himself and herself and herself and himself

and between us

there was each self and each other self, each self and each other self

and between us

Nightwalk Portfolio by Inge Morath

Raymond Barry, Tom Lillard, Jo Ann Schmidman, Ellen Maddow,
Ralph Lee, Shami Chaikin, Tina Shepard, Paul Zimet

Women's World (Jo Ann Schmidman, Ellen Maddow)

Men's World (Raymond Barry, Tom Lillard)

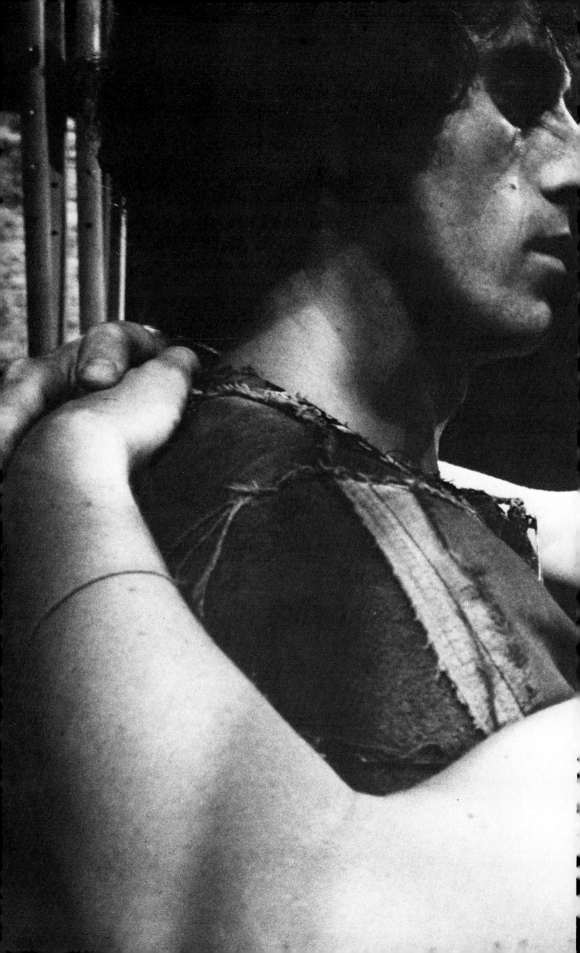

The Boss's Supper
(Above: Paul Zimet, Tina Shepard
Below: Jo Ann Schmidman, Ralph Lee,
Ellen Maddow, Raymond Barry,
Shami Chaikin, Tom Lillard)

162

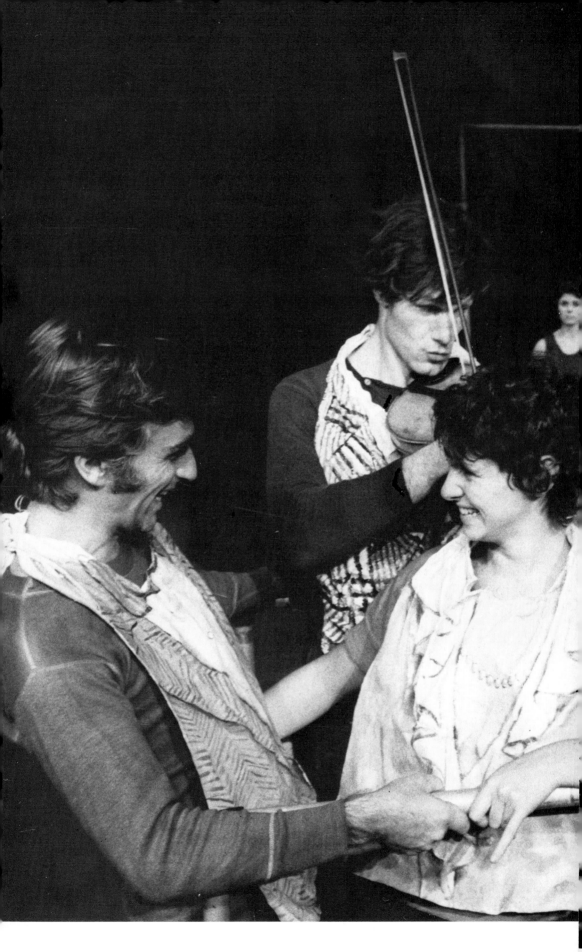

The Sleep World
(Ralph Lee, Paul Zimet,
Tina Shepard, Jo Ann Schmidman,
Ellen Maddow, Raymond Barry,
Shami Chaikin)

170

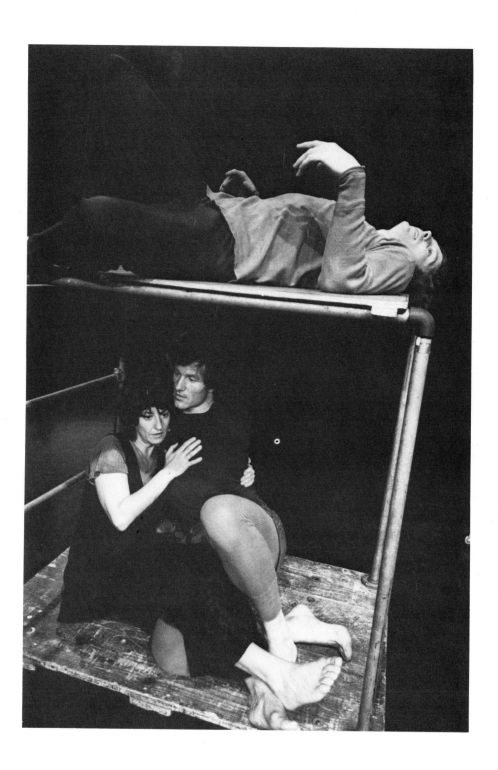

The Traveler and the Creature
(Paul Zimet, Tina Shepard)

175

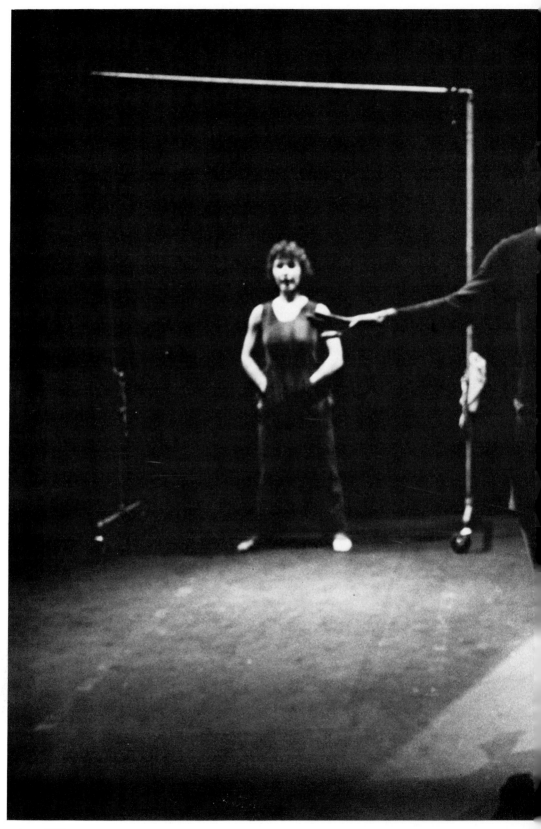

The Battle of Creatures (Tina Shepard, Raymond Barry, Paul Zimet)

Tina Shepard

182

Chronology

1963

Joseph Chaikin, then an actor in the Living Theater, calls a meeting of seventeen actors and four writers. They meet out of a dissatisfaction with the established trend of the contemporary theater. Within this new Open Theater, Chaikin begins a workshop; its members work together forming exercises and improvisations, with discussion. They enter a continuing dialogue with many people not actually members of the Open Theater, among them Gordon Rogoff, Richard Gilman, Paul Goodman, and Susan Sontag. By the end of 1963 the group begins performing publicly its improvisations and some short plays by Megan Terry, Jean-Claude van Itallie, and Bertolt Brecht at the Sheridan Square Playhouse and the Martinique Theater in New York City. "The Clown Play" from Brecht's *A Lesson in Understanding* becomes their signature piece. They continue to preform it each season until 1970.

1964-65

They continue improvisational work in a loft and perform the short plays from the previous year regularly at the Sheridan Square Playhouse and at LaMama Experimental Theater Club. They add short plays by T. S. Eliot, John Arden, Maria Irene Fornes, Sharon Thie, and others to their repertory. Workshop investigations diminish under pressure from this heavy performing schedule.

1966-67

Workshop activities increase. *Viet Rock* is performed at Yale University and off-Broadway. *Viet Rock* results from a workshop conducted by Megan Terry, the writer, and is the first full-length play developed improvisationally by a writer and the company. Members of the company also appear in Jean-Claude van Itallie's *America Hurrah*.

Fall 1967

Chaikin begins a workshop on the Bible, intending to examine the unrecorded early activities of Christ as a social anarchist. The group begins working with the Book of Genesis and explores its themes for over a year. Joseph Campbell begins the first of many talks with the company. They never develop the material on Christ but instead create *The Serpent*, with words and structure contributed by Jean-Claude van Itallie.

May 1968

The Serpent is premiered in Rome and tours throughout Italy, Germany, Switzerland, and Denmark. Alternating with *The Serpent*, the company performs an evening of political pieces entitled *Masks*, including "Eating the Corpse," "Sunday Morning," a new version of "The Clown Play," and "Wild Mountain Thyme."

January 1969

The Serpent opens in the company's loft in New York City; *Masks* is performed at various political benefits. Workshops begin on *Terminal*, co-directed by Chaikin and Roberta Sklar, with text by Susan Yankowitz.

Spring 1969

Tour of colleges in New York State. *The Serpent* and Alfred Jarry's *Ubu Cocu*, directed by Peter Feldman, are presented. Rehearsals begin for Samuel Beckett's *Endgame*, directed by Roberta Sklar. Chaikin is Hamm and Peter Maloney is Clov.

November 1969

Terminal is premiered in Bordeaux, France. The European tour continues to Paris, Berlin, and Amsterdam. The company performs *The Serpent*, *Terminal*, *Endgame*, and *Ubu Cocu*.

Spring 1970

Terminal is performed in New York City at the Washington Square Methodist Church.

Summer 1970

Members of the company go to the Santa Fe Opera, Santa Fe, New Mexico, to work with Luciano Berio on his *Opera*, which he composed based on the group's production of *Terminal*.

Fall 1970

The Open Theater reconvenes with six actors rather than fourteen. They are Raymond Barry, Shami Chaikin, Tina Shepard, Paul Zimet, Tom Lillard, and Jo Ann Schmidman. Ellen Maddow is the musician and later becomes a member of the acting company. A new workshop on the subject of human mutation is begun.

1970-71

Terminal is performed in colleges and prisons. The human mutation workshop continues.

Summer 1971

The company tours the Middle East, performing *Terminal* and *Mutations* (as a work-in-progress) in Algeria, Israel, Iran, and Yugoslavia.

Fall 1971

Back in New York, they rework *Mutations* into *The Mutation Show*.

1971

Terminal and *The Mutation Show* are performed in New York City and in colleges and prisons across the United States and Canada. The tour ends with a week-long run of *Terminal* in the Tombs (the Manhattan Men's House of Detention).

December 1972

After a seven-month hiatus, the company meets again and begins work on their new piece, starting with an investigation of the levels of sleep. Ralph Lee rejoins the company he has been absent from since *The Serpent*. Richard Giannone speaks to them about Dante; his talks help them conceive a form for *Nightwalk*. Jean-Claude van Itallie, Sam Shepard, and Megan Terry write material for the new work.

March 1972

The Mutation Show and *Nightwalk* (as a work-in-progress) are performed at The Space for Innovative Development in New York City. *Terminal* is also performed several times.

Summer 1973

The Open Theater's fifth tour outside the United States consists of performances of *The Mutation Show* and *Nightwalk* in Zurich's Theater 11; the Roundhouse Theater in London (where *Terminal* was included); and at the Holland Festival in Amsterdam, The Hague, and Nijmegen.

September-October 1973

The Open Theater performs *Terminal, The Mutation Show,* and *Nightwalk* in rotation for five weeks at St. Clement's Church in New York City. On October 16, they present *Nightwalk,* their final performance in New York.

October-December 1973

The company tours colleges across the United States with their last three works. On December 1, 1973, they end the Open Theater with a performance of *Nightwalk* at the University of California, Santa Barbara.

THE OPEN THEATER
A Beginning Bibliography
by Alex Gildzen

The volume of words written about the Open Theater can only be estimated. The company's international reputation, heightened by numerous European tours, complicates any attempt at exact measurement. But much of what was written has been preserved by the company. The Open Theater Archives, housed in the special collections department of the Kent State University Libraries, is doubtless the most complete gathering of those words.

This bibliography — selected primarily from published material in the company's archives — doesn't try to be complete. Rather it directs the reader to a blend of documents produced by members of the Open Theater and the commentaries of its contemporary reviewers.

GENERAL

Belville, Lance. "A Trip of the Open Theater; a true-to-life-if-nothing-else play in one miserable act," *WIN* (15 November 1971) 22-25.

A commentary on the company's tour of Algeria, Israel, Iran and Yugoslavia.

Brustein, Robert. "Week for farewells," *The Observer Review* (10 June 1973) 35.

Brustein precedes his review of *The Mutation Show* and *Nightwalk* with a brief chronicle of the company. He sees the OT in decline following *America Hurrah* because "the writer was treated simply as another citizen in a democratic state where everybody contributed equally," resulting in "the evolution of group activity without an overview — scattered fragmentary moments that lacked a formal imagination to give them direction and point."

Chaikin, Joseph. "Chaikin Fragments," edited by Kelly Morris, *The Drama Review*, vol. 13, no. 3 (T43) (Spring 1969) 145-47.

These bits — published before *The Presence of the Actor* — give voice to both the poet and the philosopher in Chaikin.

Chaikin, Joseph. *The Presence of the Actor* (New York, Atheneum, 1972).

Although there had been numerous interviews with Chaikin and fragments of the book itself had been published, this work establishes Chaikin as America's leading theoretician of acting. The OT would not have developed without Chaikin and his book is a prerequisite to any understanding of the company.

Chaikin, Joseph. "What the Actor Does," *Performance*, vol. 1, no. 5 (March/April 1973) 56-59.

A further extension of Chaikin's acting theories.

Clurman, Harold. "Theater," *The Nation*, vol. 206, no. 11 (11 March 1968).

In reviewing "An Informal Evening with the Open Theatre," Clurman calls the ensemble "a healthy theatre expression of the moment."

Croyden, Margaret. "The Open Theater," *Lunatics, Lovers and Poets: The Contemporary Experimental Theatre* (New York, McGraw-Hill, 1974) 169-92.

Gaisner, Rhea. "Jean-Claude van Itallie: Playwright of the Ensemble: Open Theater," *The Serif*, vol. 9, no. 4 (Winter 1972) 14-17.

A former member of the company discusses the relationship between van Itallie's workshop participation and his early short plays.

Malpede, Karen [Taylor]. "The Open Theatre," *People's Theatre in Amerika* (New York, Drama Book Specialists, 1972) 234-50.

The author investigates the radical themes and structures in *The Serpent*, *Terminal* and *The Mutation Show*.

Orzel, Nick, and Michael Smith, eds. *Eight Plays from Off-Off Broadway* (Indianapolis, Bobbs-Merrill Co., 1966).

Includes the scripts of three short plays associated with the OT — Jean-Claude van Itallie's "America Hurrah," i.e., "Motel," pp. 191-99; Maria Irene Fornes' "The Successful Life of 3," pp. 205-52; and Megan Terry's "Calm Down Mother," pp. 255-81; plus a note on the company by Joseph Chaikin (pp. 201-202), reprinted in an Italian translation in *Sipario*, no. 250 (February 1967).

Pasolli, Robert. *A Book on the Open Theatre* (New York, Bobbs-Merrill Co., 1970).

The only book-length study published during the OT's lifetime. Its strength is in a cataloging of the exercises adapted and originated by the company. The history of the OT, however, has yet to be written.

Poland, Albert, and Bruce Mailman, eds. *The Off Off Broadway Book: The Plays, People, Theatre* (Indianapolis, New York, Bobbs-Merrill Co., 1972).

The capsule history of the OT (pp. lxi-lxii) is simplistic and factually misleading but the total book is an important compilation of texts and information. For instance, in the short playwright biographies we find the OT production of *The Serpent* is listed by David Rabe as an influence.

Shepard, Sam. *Hawk Moon, A Book of Short Stories, Poems and Monologues* (Los Angeles, Black Sparrow Press, 1973).

Includes "Voices from the Dead (Monologues written for the Open Theatre 1969)," pp. 88-91.

Smith, Michael, "Theatre journal," *The Village Voice* (18 October 1973) 71.

A reminiscence by one of the OT's first playwrights.

Terry, Megan. *Viet Rock and Other Plays* (New York, Simon and Schuster, 1967).

In his introduction Richard Schechner discusses the playwright's work in relationship to the OT. The text includes "Keep Tightly Closed in a Cool Dry Place," pp. 153-98, and reprints from the *Tulane Drama Review* Peter Feldman's "Notes from the Open Theatre Production," pp. 199-206.

van Itallie, Jean-Claude. "Playwright at Work: Off Off-Broadway," *Tulane Drama Review* vol. 10, no. 4 (Summer 1966) 154-58.

The playwright recounts his joining the company and the effect of their explorations on his early work.

van Itallie, Jean-Claude. *War and Four Other Plays* (New York, Dramatists Play Service, 1967).

Includes "The Hunter and the Bird," pp. 23-29, "Almost Like Being," pp. 31-40, and "I'm Really Here," pp. 41-50.

Wagner, Phyllis Jane. "Jean-Claude van Itallie: Political Playwright," *The Serif*, vol. 9, no. 4 (Winter 1972) 19-74.

Although a discussion of only one aspect of van Itallie's work, this article provides an insight into the relationship between the company and a playwright. The author makes heavy use of her excellent interview with van Itallie.

Wagner, Phyllis Jane. *Megan Terry: Political Playwright* (University of Denver, August 1972).

A doctoral dissertation that traces the development of Terry's political consciousness. Chapter 3 investigates her relationship with the OT (1963-1966). It includes discussions of "Calm Down Mother," "Keep Tightly Closed in a Cool Dry Place," "The Magic Realists," "Comings and

Goings," and *Viet Rock*. Sources include personal correspondence and an interview with the playwright.

THE SERPENT

Hardwick, Elizabeth. "Scalp!" *New York Review of Books* (6 November 1969) 39-40.

The critic labels OT's *The Serpent* "a soft, sentimental work, sadly trivial and banal."

Kerr, Walter. "What If Cain Did Not Know How to Kill Abel," *New York Times*, section 2 (9 February 1969) 1, 8.

Kerr is awed by the power of the piece's image of the first murder. He also calls the ensemble the best of its kind because it has humor and respects both word and gesture. The piece is reprinted as the opening section of the title essay in Kerr's *God on the Gymnasium Floor and Other Theatrical Adventures* (New York, Simon and Schuster, 1971).

Lahr, John. "The Open Theatre: Beyond the Absurd," *Evergreen Review*, vol. 13, no. 66 (May 1969) 63-68.

Lahr sees *The Serpent* as an attempt to use myth to combat the despair of the existential philosophy of the absurd and as an affirmation of the life force. A slightly revised version, retitled "The Open Theater's *Serpent*," is in Lahr's *Up Against the Fourth Wall* (New York, Grove Press, 1970), 158-74.

Lahr, John, and Jonathan Price, eds. *The Great American Life Show: 9 Plays from the Avant-garde Theater* (New York, Bantam Books, 1974).

This paperback anthology reprints *The Serpent* with an introduction by Lahr (in which he dubs the OT "the most ruthlessly experimental of the American theaters") and excerpts from van Itallie's 20 February 1970 letter on how *not* to perform the piece.

Lane, John Francis. "Theater: The U.S. influence," *Naples Daily American* (9 May 1968).

Description of the OT's first public performance of *The Serpent* in Rome.

Mohan, Roberta Newcomer. *The Open Theater Production of* The Serpent. A Ceremony: *An Examination of Aesthetic Purpose and Creative Process* (Kent State University, December 1973).

This master's thesis traces the process of creating *The Serpent*. Of particular interest is a chapter on the Bible workshop incorporating in addition to previously published sources the log kept by Kenneth Glickfeld and the author's interview with Tina Shepard who created the role of Eve.

van Itallie, Jean-Claude. *The Serpent. A Ceremony written by Jean-Claude van Itallie in collaboration with the Open Theater under the direction of Joseph Chaikin* (New York, Atheneum, 1969).

The finished script plus "From the Playwright," pp. ix-xi, and "From the Director," pp. xii-xviii.

TERMINAL

Lahr, John. "On-stage," *The Village Voice* (23 April 1970) 43.

"In dramatizing death so clinically," writes Lahr, "the Open Theatre aspires to renew the audience's sense of life and the need for compassionate change." The column is reprinted as "Open Theatre's *Terminal*," pp. 201-204, in Lahr's *Astonish Me: Adventures in Contemporary Theater* (New York, Viking Press, 1973).

Ryan, Paul Ryder. "*Terminal*: An Interview with Roberta Sklar," *The Drama Review*, vol. 15, no. 3a (T-51) (Summer 1971) 149-57.

The work's co-director discusses the origin of *Terminal* and its intention: "We wanted to meet with the spectator around the same issues that we had met with one another for a year — the assumption that there is a prescribed attitud toward death, that there is a prescribed way of dealing with it, which is *not* dealing with it."

Sainer, Arthur. "The judgment," *The Village Voice* (13 May 1971).

In this discussion of *Terminal* in terms of process, Sainer sees the piece's limitations as a failure to deal with spiritual dignity, the soul, afterlife.

Schevill, James. "The Open Theatre and *Terminal,*" *Break Out! In Search of New Theatrical Environments* (Chicago, Swallow Press, 1973) 336-42.

Schevill considers his reactions to *Terminal*, using the piece as a basis for observations on experimental theater. He views the OT as a possible model for the theater of the future — "small groups of actors, playwrights, and directors working together towards a common goal" — but warns against what he sees as an abstract quality in group-produced work lacking "real characters."

Williams, Tom. *"Terminal:* Twelve Scenes on Death," *Dramatics*, vol. 44, no. 3 (December 1972): 10-12.

A student describes a high school production of *Terminal.*

Yankowitz, Susan. "*Terminal.* A collective work created by the Open Theater ensemble co-directed by Joseph Chaikin and Roberta Sklar," *Scripts* 1, no. 1 (November 1971) 17-45.

First publication of the text.

THE MUTATION SHOW

Kareda, Urjo. "New York's Open Theatre gives a startling performance," *The Toronto Star* (12 February 1972).

The reviewer calls the company "as brilliant and breath-taking as sudden lightning on a dead night" in this enlightened review of *The Mutattion Show.*

Lahr, John. "On-stage," *The Village Voice* (30 March 1972) 54, 77.

Reprinted as "Open Theatre's *The Mutation Show,*" pp. 205-10, in *Astonish Me: Adventures in Contemporary Theatre* (New York, Viking Press, 1973).

Malpede, Karen [Taylor]. "Two Kaspars," *Performance*, vol. 1, no. 6 (May/June 29-35.

A comparison of Peter Handke's play *Kaspar* and the Open Theater's *The Mutation Show.*

Sainer, Arthur. "Words from the West (2)," *The Village Voice* (27 April 1972) 73.

A review of the Berkeley performance: "It's a marvelous work, the freest, most joyful creation that the ensemble has involved itself in since its inception in 1963."

Wardle, Irving. "Characters and effects in bizarre mutations," *The London Times* (6 June 1973) 11.

The critic misses the "linear pattern" a playwright would impose on the work's images but — unlike the majority of London critics — finds it "an arresting piece of work."

NIGHTWALK

Gussow, Mel. "Open Theater Offers Abstract 'Nightwalk,'" *New York Times* (11 September 1973) 55.

The first major American review of the ensemble's final work.

Sainer, Arthur. "A walk among outer humans," *The Village Voice* (13 September 1973), 66.

Sainer's quarrel with the piece is that the humans lack the nobility of the birds.

Wardle, Irving. "Open Theatre/Round House," *The London Times* (8 June 1973) 11.

The review focuses on the OT's "comic inheritance."